BEATRIX POTTER

Her Lakeland Years

W. R. Mitchell

Great Northern Books
PO Box 213, Ilkley, LS29 9WS
www.greatnorthernbooks.co.uk

ISBN: 978 1 905080 71 7

Design and layout: David Burrill

CIP Data
A catalogue for this book is available from the British Library

Contents

Over: Lakeland Life (painting by David Hoyle, courtesy of the author)

Beatrix Potter in her 'quaint dress', photographed at Hill Top in 1913 with her dog Kep. (photo courtesy Victoria & Albert Museum)

About this book ...

This is the third book based on the recollections of Lakeland folk. In 1987, the author published *Beatrix Potter Remembered*, subtitled *Her Life in Lakeland*. In 1998, a fuller account appeared under the title *Beatrix Potter: Her Life in the Lake District*. The present book takes in much social history and, importantly in the context of a remarkable woman, her regard for Lakeland farming. It amounted to great affection for the tough little Herdwick breed of sheep.

In a foreword to the 1998 edition, Judy Taylor wrote: "Sadly, the small band of people who met and knew Beatrix Potter is fast dwindling, which makes Bill Mitchell's interviews, which he began in 1955 and has often transcribed into the dialect of the area, into snippets of history. They provide us with a realistic and down-to-earth picture of what the people of the Lake District thought of this woman from London, who not only chose to make her home amongst them for thirty years but also competed with them in their traditional farming life. The fact that everyone does not agree adds considerably to the interest and entertainment."

As a foreword to the 1987 edition, Mary Burkett, who then presided over Abbot Hall at Kendal, had observed that Beatrix Potter's name bears with it an air of mystery because it brings with it associations of a scientist, a sheep-farmer, an intellectual as well as that of an inspired illustrator and author of children's tales: "Many books have been written about her stating emphatically what sort of person she was. But since then a secret diary has come to light which reveals her as an even more enigmatic figure.

"She achieved a style of animal painting which is remarkable not only in its simplicity and purity but in its lack of sentimentality. The animals are, in spite of their clothes, tough little creatures and her awareness of form and action is clearly shown in their obvious character.

"Her popularity, however, increases all the time. When we staged our

Beatrix Potter with a prize card for Herdwick sheep (painting by Janet Rawlins)

first exhibition of her work at Abbot Hall in February and March 1986, we had more people visiting the gallery then than we had in mid-summer despite the weather. Always people want to know what sort of person she really was. There are still some people in the Lake District who remember her, and even a few who worked for her.

"This anthology of people's memories of her will add to the ever-increasing store of information about her. It is an excellent idea of Bill Mitchell, the author, to have accumulated these recollections of thirty or more years of her life and I wish it every success."

First Impressions

She was so great in her tiny way. She was a little bundle of charm and cleverness and great wisdom.
Josephina Banner

Behind that quaint dress and bent head there was a very beautiful character.
Annie Black, of Sawrey

Under a tight little knitted bonnet was a face that had the complexion of a child's, with lovely rosy cheeks. She always looked alive and jolly...
William H Waddington, artist, who saw Beatrix almost every day.

Mrs Heelis wore a trilby hat. A *man's* trilby hat!
Mrs Birkett, of Elterwater, watching Beatrix arrive at Grasmere in her chauffeur-driven car.

She had dark brown, rather frizzy hair and a round face with a lovely complexion for an old lady.
Tom Storey.

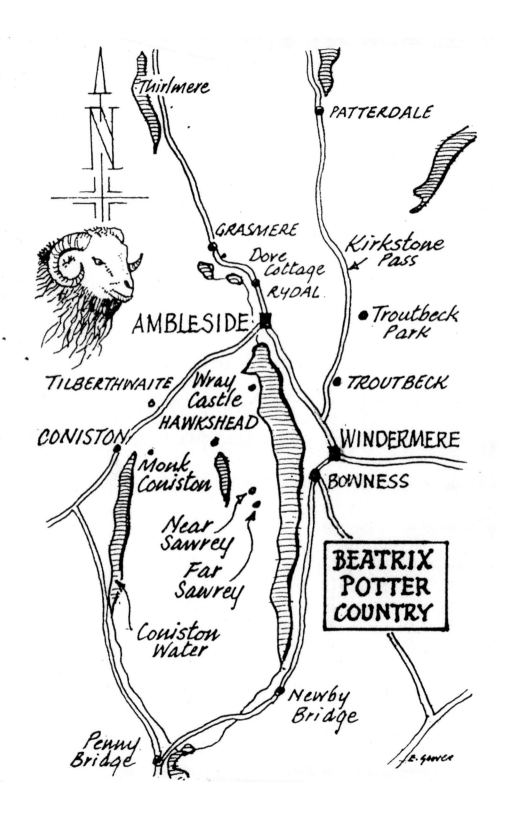

1: Looking for Beatrix

She entered my life in childhood. Glancing through Beatrix Potter's twenty little books, with their bright illustrations and simple text, I was introduced to a host of fanciful but entertaining characters. A rabbit wore a blue coat to go to a party. A hedgehog took in washing. A frog, out fishing, was almost eaten by a trout. Cats kept house for tailors. A duck had a sore throat because – it was suggested – too much time was being spent with its head in water.

My interest in recording Beatrix's associations with the Lake District, where she spent the last thirty years of her life, began with a chance meeting with an old lady in the 1950s. I had become editor of the magazine *Cumbria*, part of a publishing company that operated from a double-fronted house at the Yorkshire village of Clapham. Living just round the corner was the Richards family. Annie (nee Black), who had been reared at Sawrey, near Hawkshead, in the southern part of the Lake District, casually remarked: "I remember Beatrix Potter." And I realised, inspirationally, that if Annie could remember Beatrix, others in her chosen area of Lakeland would be able to recall the world's best-known children's author who lived in "the pleasant unchanging world of realism and romance."

Annie recalled Beatrix as a small lady, somewhat tubby, with rounded shoulders, silky white hair and a fresh-looking face. Her eyes were a brilliant blue. She wore clothes of homespun wool, with two huge patch pockets. The skirt, extending to her ankles, revealed an inch or two of worsted stockings, "a kind of heather mixture". Her straw hat was held in place by black tape tied under her chin.

A workaday Beatrix had donned an apron made of sacking and clattered about Sawrey village wearing – clogs! Small children, scared at her strange appearance and manners, flattened themselves against the walls as she went by. "If they were making a noise – as kiddies do – she would tell them about it, till they got scared of her." To older folk who saw her regularly, she was socially indifferent and somewhat eccentric. She never conversed with children she met. In a village like

Sawrey, where anyone who appeared unfriendly was regarded as strange, it was best to avoid them.

Annie's family lived outside the village and father was surprised – shocked indeed – to receive a message from Beatrix more or less commanding him to send his son and daughter to Hill Top, her first local home. Here they would receive the gift of a book. Each child must be clean and tidy, carrying a linen bag in which the book would be kept clean. Children of school age got the same invitation. And, said Annie, "there were threats and tears, for we did not want to go."

Beatrix proved to be kind and pleasant. "We were told to take care of the books," said Annie. "Mine was *The Tale of Two Bad Mice* and my brother was handed *The Tale of Peter Rabbit.*" When the Black family emigrated to Western Canada, Annie tucked memories of Beatrix Potter at the back of her mind until she realised that Canadian children were "going mad" about her mini-books. "If I told anyone I knew her, they wanted to know about the appearance of the lovely lady. All I could answer was: 'She's a queer old thing.' They insisted she must be lovely."

On the Black family's return to Sawrey, a year or two later, Beatrix looked stranger than before. On moving into a cottage that stood in Beatrix's farmyard, they began to know her true self. "Behind that quaint dress and bent head there was a very beautiful character. Even my father began to think there was 'nowt much wrang' with her after all." She showed many kindnesses towards Annie's parents.

On the day Dick Black died she asked if she could see him. Annie took her upstairs to the bedroom where he had been laid out. "When I turned the sheet back from my dead father's face, she knelt down and wept, saying: 'I've always respected you. God bless you'." Farming was her obsession now. She dressed in old clothes. "No-one would have termed her 'lovely lady' now." She could be waspish. On the day when Annie's mother painted the door of the cottage dark green – with two white panels! – there was an immediate rebuke. Beatrix did not want her houses to be so adorned.

Though strict, she could be generous. The Blacks moved into a cottage near Castle Cottage, her marital home. An adjoining orchard was stocked with apple and plum trees. Beatrix told the Black children: "They are my fruit trees. I don't want you to help yourselves but I have given you one apple and one plum tree. I have put a red band round them. You can have the fruit from those two trees." It was, said Annie, "much nicer to have fruit still on a tree than to be given a basketful."

Tom Storey, her shepherd, admitted that she could be "rather funny" with children. "I had a little boy and girl when I came down to these parts. She thought the world of the boy and she didn't like the girl. The reason why she liked the boy was probably because he was keen on farming, though only four years old." Beatrix looked like a farmer but her voice was cultured and refined, with no trace of dialect. According to Tom, she was especially fond of old people. When she did a good deed – as was occasionally the case – it was done quietly. Very few folk got to know about it.

What was the secret of the astonishing array of stories that poured from Beatrix Potter's pen every time she put it to paper, from the first illustrated letter to a poorly

Windermere Ferry, viewed from what used to be the Westmorland shore.

child in September, 1893 (bringing Peter Rabbit into being) to a final letter to a friend in 1934, when she declared: "I am written out for story books and my eyes are tired for painting"?

She was twenty-seven years of age when she began writing. She put down her pen at the age of fifty-eight. Into those forty years she poured out letters, paintings and rhymes to the delight of children all over the world. It was all done for pleasure. Beatrix could not bear the notion of "writing to order".

Margaret Lane's *The Tale of Beatrix Potter*, written in 1946, inspired Leslie Linder to begin, in 1951, a twenty-year spell of research into Beatrix Potter, first as an artist, then as a diarist; her journals were kept using a secret code of cipher-writing. Linder, tenacious and patient, broke the code. His transcription was published as *The Journal of Beatrix Potter* in 1966. There followed a well-illustrated tome, entitled *A History of the Writings of Beatrix Potter*, extending to almost 450 pages. Perhaps the key sentence in this book is from her letter to an American woman friend. Beatrix wrote: "I have just made stories to please myself because I never grew up."

Having listened to the tales of Annie Richards, it was time for me to visit Near Sawrey, which has an enchanted setting beside Esthwaite Water. I approached from Bowness, using the Windermere ferry on its six-minute crossing of the narrows of the great lake. We sailed from Ferry Nab to a beach below Ferry House, which in Beatrix's time was a hotel. The Potter family patronised it when prospecting for a summer holiday place in South Lakeland.

An early ferryboat was fitted with a boiler and engine on the starboard side while on the port side lay a large anchor and lifeboat for use in case of emergencies. A single cable connected the boat with each shoreline, adding to the risk of the craft breaking free. The ferry I first used would have been familiar to Beatrix. It was coal-powered. A tall, relatively thin, Woodbine-type funnel emitted some soot. Fussy passengers undertook some surreptitious dry-cleaning. Two cables were strung from bank to bank to keep the ferry under control. A lady passenger thought the cables were holding up rather than keeping the craft to a fixed route. Anxiously, she asked: "If one cable snaps, will the boat sink?"

Jack Bowman, ferryman, told me that an impending South Country visitor to the area wished to book a berth. She was unaware that the ferry's crossing lasted from two to three minutes. When Jack, nobbut a lad, began work on the ferry, a drove of ponies that were being driven to market bore down on the craft from the Lancashire side. Jack should have stretched a chain across the far end of the ferry to keep the ponies on board. Instead, scared, he shut himself in a cabin. The ponies, having cantered noisily across the deck, with nothing to impede them, fell into the lake!

As one of the lake steamers passed, twixt Lakeside, Bowness Bay and Waterhead, I was told the amusing tale of a freshwater sailor. A distraught passenger mentioned to one of the crew of a steamer he had accidentally dropped his watch over the side. The sailor promised to recover it "when we clean the lake out at the back-end of the year." The incredulous passenger could not believe a vast lake like Windermere was regularly cleaned out. Pointing to the hills flanking the lake, the sailor said: "That's where we put t'muck."

On my visit to Beatrix Potter Country, the ferry left a herring-bone wake on a calm lake. This being autumn, the well-wooded hills were brooding in a light-grey mist. The countryside wore its Joseph's coat of many colours. Among the poets who distinguished the pages of *Cumbria* with her work was Edna M Cass. Bewitched by moonlight on a summer's night, she wrote of -

The lake, a looking glass for fairy queens,
The ferry boat, a dainty bark canoe,
Starting a voyage to far distant scenes.
Should we go too?
And land where little woodland folks were born,
Where Peter Rabbit's parties came to life,
And Mr Dormouse scurries through the corn
To fetch his wife.

Tern, a graceful little steamboat on Windermere.

Swan approaches the pier at the foot of Windermere.

A chimney pot at Near Sawrey with a weathervane featuring Jemima Puddleduck.

The poem ends:

To influence all life with just a story,
But right that one with such a tale to tell
Should choose Far Sawrey.

Beatrix winced during the 1930s when strident noises were being heard on Windermere. Locally made hydroplanes zoomed up and down the lake. A hydroplane, like a giant wooden shoe, with an outward-bound engine, was streamlined, adapted for skimming the water under power. Various designs were being tried by the boat-builders of Bowness Bay. One type touched the water only in two places, each merely the size of a hand.

In a letter to the Editor of *Country Life*, Beatrix observed that everyone used the ferry. "On calm summer waters no voyage is more cheerful and pleasant than this crossing of Windermere. Those who live to the west can tell another tale of winter nights, when the ferry cannot cross in the teeth of the wind. Then the home-coming carriers are storm-stayed at Bowness, and the Crier of Claife calls in vain for the ferryman." Now, however, "our peaceful lake is disturbed by the presence of a hydroplane...A more inappropriate place for experimenting with flying machines could scarcely be chosen." Her letter received editorial support. The hydroplane production continued.

Beatrix was most certainly familiar with the story of The Crier of Claife, a demon ferryman who claimed men's souls, shouting "Ferry Ho!" on wild nights. A ferryman who answered the call was found, next

Beswick advert for Beatrix Potter characters.

morning, speechless and almost insane from shock. John Edward Atkinson, a long-time ferryman, told me of a passenger who, when the ferry grated to a halt, bid him goodnight. Immediately afterwards, John heard a splash. The passenger had walked in the wrong direction. An early motorist did not see why, if a steam engine could float across the lake, a petrol engine shouldn't. He gave up the attempt when the water was up to his shoulders!

On that first venture into Beatrix Potter Country, I had pocketed a copy of Beatrix's diminutive *Tale of Benjamin Bunny*, dedicated to the children of Sawrey. From the 1890s, her drawings of rabbits and mice had been used by a London firm for their Christmas cards. Her first book, *The Tale of Peter Rabbit*, was published privately in December, 1901. Astonishingly, it had been rejected by six publishing firms, including Warnes. The print run was 250 and the illustrations were in monochrome.

Warnes subsequently did a U-turn, printing the book with the illustrations rendered in colour. The 8,000 copies of the original print were soon taken up. Book royalties eventually made a fortune for Beatrix. In 1947, after her death, Beswick pottery produced a series of models based on Beatrix Potter characters. The original idea came from the wife of the managing director, who had just returned from a Lakeland holiday. The first figure to appear was – Jemima Puddleduck.

As I trudged up Ferry Hill, I recalled a story that when Beatrix Potter was on this hill on a wild, wet day, she was briefly accompanied by a tramp. Mistaking her – in her dowdy clothes - for one of the nomadic fraternity, he remarked: "Ee, it's a dirty day for the likes of you and me to be on t'road, missus." Two hamlets, named Far and Near in their relation to Hawkshead, lay in rich countryside with a backdrop of the Tilberthwaite Fells, beyond which was glorious Langdale..

The trim little farmhouses and cottages, which were whitewashed, gleamed in sunshine. This halcyon period of Lakeland life was the calm before the transformation wrought by mass tourism and a stultifying web of bureaucracy. In a farming revolution, fields bedecked with wildflowers would be transformed into tracts of lush green.

Gentle Shorthorn cattle – dual-purpose, noted for both milk and beef – would give way before an invasion of black-and-white Friesians, originating in the Low Countries. An old Lakeland chap, in a reference to milking, disrespectfully called them "watter-cans"! I heard the *clip-clop* of a horse's hooves. In a world tenanted mainly by sheep, the Kendal Rough would yield to the ubiquitous Swaledale breed, though the old custom of overwintering young Herdwicks on low ground or even on sea-washed marshes would continue – for a time. Beatrix loved the Herdwick breed.

The name Sawrey is said to be derived from Sawrayes, a muddy area. It has long been in a countryside associated with the Sandys family. Beatrix described the village as lying in "the very pretty hill country." It was "not wild like Keswick or Ullswater." From the woods came the gruff bark of a testy roebuck. Roe of the reddish Austrian strain had been introduced to the wooded hills of Claife, in the township of which

Opposite page: A herd of cattle, collected for milking.

Right: Figure in a garden at Near Sawrey.

the Sawreys lay. South Lakeland held a remnant population of the old Furness reds, the finest free-ranging deer in the land.

In those quiet days of the 1950s, I stood on the shore of Esthwaite Water, beside which the Potter family rented spacious accommodation and lazed away the summer. Esthwaite, the smallest of the great lakes, is a stretch of mirror-like water a mere one a-half miles in length – the most changed of the Cumbrian lakes, transformed because of its relative shallowness and the farming round about it.

Mr Potter's main interest during his Lakeland holidays at Sawrey was in angling. Fred Coward, who in the 1950s was water bailiff for Esthwaite Estates, and had two boats for hire, told me that when the

lake froze over in a cold snap it became a rink for local skaters. Fred had an encyclopaedic mind and a retentive memory.

With from ten to twelve streams flowing into the lake, the fish stock is well-fed and healthy. Rain on the fells washes down all kinds of tasty food. At one time, eels were trapped as they left the lake heading for their spawning grounds across the Atlantic. In my time, Cunsey Beck, the lake's outlet, had been dredged by the Lancashire River Board. The Sandys family of Graythwaite, owners of the lake, had a concrete bed made hereabouts, planks being set across the outlet during the summer season to keep up the level of the lake.

Fred said that in recent times, bream and roach had been counted among the fish caught by anglers. These fish may have come from Priest's Pond during flood time. Anglers used to bring cans of roach as bait for the pike. They were in the habit of tipping spare roach into Priest's Pond, and here the fish bred. I asked Fred about the pike and heard that recently a twenty-pounder had been landed. There were some lively perch, making the scales dip at half a pound to two pounds.

In the quiet and restful air of the *Tower Bank Arms*, at Sawrey, Margaret Burns gave me her impressions of Beatrix. "I saw her every day. We often chatted under an old apple tree they cut down last year. There's no two ways about it – she was a character. I liked her very much but, mind you, if anyone got on the wrong side of her I don't think they ever got back into her favour again. I used to either say nothing or side with her. It was the best way."

One night, when there was a sing-song in the *Tower Bank Arms*, and - being a John Peel anniversary – Lakeland hunting songs were popular, Beatrix refused to enter the building. She was seen pacing up and down outside, listening to the music! Her daughter, Willow Taylor, recalled that Beatrix entered the hotel "only when she wanted to tell my father that I'd been a naughty girl!"

The Postlethwaites, of High Green Gate, were near neighbours of William and Beatrix Heelis. Their daughter, Amanda, recalled her first memory of Beatrix. "I suppose I was only about six years old at the time. She was walking down the road and seemed to be wrapped in sacks. She had a bit of a hat on. I thought: 'What a funny old woman.' She just walked down the road, looking at everything, grunting with disapproval at this and that..."

Amanda worked for four years in the small grocery shop owned by the Taylor family, John – the original owner - being the local joiner and wheelwright. The shop, situated in Smithy Lane, achieved immortality when, in the autumn of 1908, Beatrix wrote about it in *Ginger and Pickles*. The doings of a tom-cat and a terrier, whose customers were mainly rabbits and mice, were set against a backdrop of recognisable village scenes.

In real life, Beatrix was a regular customer at Taylors' shop. She'd probably need some sugar, having run short, or some sweets. The shop windows had small panes. The door was approached down a passage and the shop itself was not much bigger than the living room of a house. Flour was kept in an oak chest. Herbs and spices were in small wooden drawers. Said Amanda: "You'd see bacon hanging up. We cut lard to demand." It was not a business success. "People bought Jack-o'-the-pinch [items they had run out of]. The little shop eventually had to close."

At Easter, in the Sawrey of Beatrix's day, hard-boiled eggs were dyed using a time-honoured method involving onion skins or cochineal. They were rolled on steep hillsides on Easter Monday and, when shattered, were eaten. Easterledge pudding was made from bistort which grew locally. It might also be boiled and consumed as a vegetable. Children played games such as rounders on a roadway where traffic was spasmodic.

Amanda Thistlethwaite, née Postlethwaite, who regularly met Beatrix.

Fred Satterthwaite presided over the smithy. I heard of two ladies – Mesdames Taylor and Chapman – who sported bushy beards.

High Green Gate, Sawrey, home to the Postlethwaites.
Opposite: Tower Bank Arms at Near Sawrey, which Beatrix
passed on her daily walks.

Amanda gave me a photograph of one of them. Fields that now are numbered on the map were known by descriptive names such as Bull Banks. On this particular field, which belonged to Beatrix, local folk gathered in the 1930s to celebrate the Coronation of George V.

I bed-and-breakfasted at a roadside house near Hawkshead (an old market town known to local folk as Arksh'd). The only available bedroom held a single, iron-framed bed. There was so little spare room that when I stretched I felt simultaneous pressure on my head and feet! Next morning I stepped from bed on to chilling linoleum and, with a six-inch shiver, dressed hurriedly and breakfasted in a room heated by a paraffin lamp.

Breakfast featured eggs laid by the hens that twitched and clucked in the neighbouring croft. I tasted home-cured ham within slices of home-baked bread. Refreshed and replete, and with the Potter book still in my pocket, I strode through a little town with every feature of which Beatrix was familiar.

Hawkshead occupies part of the green floor of Esthwaite vale, between wooded hills, close to the geological sump of the valley – the aforementioned Esthwaite Water. Some historians believe that the name of this settlement was derived from the place where a Norseman called Haukr abided. An enterprising businessman called his cafe and restaurant *The Norseman*. Was the stockaded settlement of Old Haukr on the green mound now occupied by the parish church? I like to think so.

Beatrix's curiosity must have led her to a little historical research. Hawkshead's formative years were in the boom period for English wool, when Kendal proclaimed that "wool is my bread" and received packhorse loads of wool from the hinterland. The Hawkshead consignments would go by way of the Windermere ferry.

Standing by the church, which has traces of Norman times, I beheld a cluster of buildings with colour or white-washed walls and slate roofs. Architecturally, it looked a huddle, with buildings standing close together as though for mutual protection. Hawkshead has its satellite hamlets – Roger Ground, Colthouse and Outgate. Among the old – and very large – local families were the Cowards and the Wrights, Shuttleworths, Murphys and Dixons.

A solicitors' office became familiar to Beatrix in 1908 when she sought the advice of W H Heelis & Son, whose practice took in Hawkshead and Ambleside. At the former village were two partners – William Dickenson Heelis and his son William Heelis. To distinguish them, local

The Postlethwaite family at Sawrey, photographed by Beatrix.

A Hawkshead side street in high summer.
Opposite: Hawkshead, viewed from the churchyard.

Main Street, Hawkshead.

people knew the former as Hawkshead Willy and the latter, because of family associations with the Eden Valley, as Appleby Bill.

Willie Heelis became the dutiful husband of Beatrix, who consequently was a regular visitor, clad in a felt hat, cape, long dress and rather large and "serviceable" footwear. Her straight-backed Wolseley car, driven by Walter Stevens, was instantly recognisable. It passed unimpeded through the constrictions of the village.

In the 1930s, a time of industrial depression, many families entered a period of relative prosperity, catering for those who arrived by car, which was no longer a toy just for the well-to-do but a means of transport for the thrifty members of the working class. At Bank Holiday times, PS Waring mustered three constables. They were on duty in the main street, attempting to control the traffic, human traffic lights who permitted northward progress for a while, then gave priority to southbound traffic. "If a motor coach and a Ribble bus met, that was that!"

The oldest folk remembered when Pape's horse-drawn coaches arrived from Keswick via the Ferry. The Brown family had a service from Ambleside. Missis Garnett, the postmistress, owned a horse-drawn wagonette that was available for hire. (She also kept the horse-drawn hearse). John Coward, who built the local garage in 1933, used a cab to collect holidaymakers from the railway station in Windermere.

Beatrix was familiar with every street, alley, alcove and square. She would know an architectural curiosity - a hillside home supported on one side by stilts. Hawkshead has a large 15th century church and a tiny Victorian chapel. A grammar school, founded by a member of the Sandys family, was attended by William Wordsworth. The Market Hall, grandly known as the Town Hall, contained a prison cell, with a stout door topped by an iron grill to admit some air to a cupboard-like space beyond. Old-time troublemakers were given short shrift.

I soon had the impression that Hawkshead folk were fond of their stomachs. As one of them said: "It's your stomach that holds your back up!" In a local guide book, written in 1928, when Beatrix Potter was in

Opposite: An old lady noted for making tasty Hawkshead 'wiggs'.
Right: Brenda Seddon with a tray of freshly-baked 'wiggs'.

her Lakeland glory, I read a paragraph about local food. Oat bread or cake –known locally as clap bread - was still being made and it was considered excellent to finish your lunch with butter and cheese.

Hawkshead Cake, a thin flat "pastry" nearly a foot across and filled with a sugary and succulent packing of currants, was made using a recipe brought to Hawkshead about eighty years before by a Liverpool woman. Sweet pie was a Christmas dish compounded of fat mutton, raisins, currants, sugar and spice, covered all over with puff pastry.

Hawkshead *wiggs* – a word used by Pepys in 1664 – were tea cakes, about four inches long and three inches wide. They were made using caraway seeds, not currants, and were described to me as being "nice and brown on top". Fascinated by the delicacy known as *wiggs*, I inquired about it from local people and heard about Mary Noble, who had died almost half a century before my visit but was remembered as the aged maker of *wiggs*, which she sold in her little shop, along with snuff and tobacco! When a sheep fair was held at Hawkshead, Mary Noble made "fair cakes", a variation on *wiggs*. The cakes were round and contained currants. She also made funeral cakes. The Noble family were thrifty, making their own paper bags out of newspaper.

In 1951, I had chatted with Mrs Alice Black, then ninety-two years of age. Within easy memory were special events held at Hawkshead public houses. Admission was paid for and a fiddler provided the music. Local publicans were enterprising in those days. One of them charged people to see an old, shapeless clog which he kept in a glass case. Clogs were the type of footwear that appealed to Beatrix Potter when undertaking workaday jobs.

Alice had a rich fund of memories. When Mrs Black was married at Hawkshead, she and her husband travelled by coach and four to Keswick for a honeymoon. A tame trout, said to be black as coal, inhabited a trough near Fold Cottage, her first home after marriage. Loaves of bread were distributed at church to the poor of the parish. The priest handed them through a small window.

In the mid-19th century, when there were few toilets locally, Mrs Black's grandmother built three and rented them to local folk half yearly. Each tenant received a large key to the allocated toilet. The key was attached by cord to bobbins. In the days before doctors and district nurses were common in Lakeland, Mrs Black was not above helping children into the world. I asked her if she helped with many, and she replied, with a chuckle: "Very near all Sawrey."

It was through Mrs Black that I first heard of charcoal burning, which took place widely in coppice-wooded South Lakeland. Beatrix Potter was doubtless familiar with a whiff of smoke from slow-burning mounds composed of wood and covered evenly with soil to prevent the fire bursting into flame and ruining the charcoal. Mr Black was a charcoal-burner. He was eight years old when he was first involved with the craft and he worked until he was about sixty-five. When there was a "burn", his family saw him only on Sunday. He would set off to work at 4 am and on summer nights it was often 10 pm when he returned. Sometimes he walked from Sawrey to Langdale and back, a round trip of about twenty-eight miles.

When the actual burning of the felled and neatly-arranged pieces of wood took place, a charcoal-burner might be away from his home for weeks. These Men of the Woods lived in primitive huts constructed from birchwood, returning home periodically to replenish their stock of food. Mr Black kept his food in an old tin trunk.

The fires, which were known as *pits*, were built up with a stout piece of wood down the middle. The fire was covered with sod and soil, the process being set when the central stick was removed and into the void went burning embers. The wood was permitted to smoulder, never burst into flame, for the prescribed number of hours. The fire was then extinguished with water and the charcoal prepared for despatch to customers.

Hazel was a popular type of wood for burning. Mr Black's charcoal went mainly to the tanning factories of Dunfermline. Some of the charcoal-burners put boxes of clay pipes in the *pits*. When the charcoal was removed, the pipes were quite black. Being well and truly seasoned, they could be sold for extra money. Charcoal-burners had to be aware of the presence in these coppice woods of the adder, our only poisonous snake.

As I walked back towards the ferry, I sniffed the air but there was not a whiff of a woodland charcoal-burn. I could not understand why Beatrix Potter, a woman who had provided the children of the world with such a wonderful set of word-and-picture books should be so strange towards young folk, as the folk of Sawrey had stated. My bewilderment increased as the Windermere ferry ploughed the lake water from Lancashire back towards the Westmorland shore. Taking from my pocket *The Tale of Benjamin Bunny*, I noticed once again the dedication: FOR THE CHILDREN OF SAWREY from OLD MR BUNNY.

I had been told that Mrs Gaddum, of Burneside, who remembered Beatrix, told her friends that she was by nature a retiring person. She did not like people fussing over her, asking for her autograph or saying nice things about her books. A Hawkshead woman who bought an autographed copy lamented that her children had defaced it with scribbles. Beatrix's autograph was almost obliterated. Said the woman: "We didn't appreciate her."

Edith Gaddum, Beatrix's cousin, lived at Brockhole. (photo courtesy Brockhole)

Elterwater – historic wintering place for Icelandic whooper swans.

Beatrix most certainly had a "nice side", an example of which was regularly visiting John Taylor, an old chap who was bedridden. She asked him which was his favourite animal. Old John replied: "A dormouse." Beatrix promptly wrote her book about dormice – and dedicated it to the old man.

2: Lakeland Holidays

Helen Beatrix Potter, the only daughter of Rupert Potter and his wife Helen, was born on 28 July, 1866, at 2 Bolton Gardens, London. The Potters were not "short of brass", having inherited wealth from families who were prominent in the Lancashire textile industry. They quit Lancashire. Rupert became a barrister who had the means to leave the running of his legal practice to others.

Rupert was a regular visitor to the Reform Club, where he conversed with notable liberal thinkers. During long family holidays on rented estates, he was able to relax further and indulge his twin passions for angling and photography. His wife, a gifted amateur painter, was a London socialite with a fondness for organising elaborate dinner parties.

Her young daughter had little pride in being a Londoner. Whenever this was mentioned, she claimed it was a mistake; her mother happened to be there at the time! Walter Bertram, her brother, was born six years later. They were distinguished by the names *B* and *Bertie*. Brought up at home by Nanny or Governess, Beatrix was discouraged by her mother from having friends of a similar age to visit her. They might introduce germs into the family!

Beatrix, a weakly child, had spells of ill-health and suffered periods of depression. At home, she had the stimulus of fine paintings and a well-stocked library. Visits to her grandparents' country house at Hatfield in Hertfordshire and its associated 300-acre estate nurtured her interest in the countryside and biology.

When the Potters had long holidays, in Perthshire and the English Lake District, Miss McKenzie, a young Scottish nurse, fired Beatrix's imagination with stories about supernatural beings – about witches and elves — who were said to inhabit the glens and hills of Scotland. Beatrix, an avid notetaker, studied fungus and fossils. She dissected dead animals, then drew or painted them.

The summer of 1871 was spent at Dalguise House, near Dunkeld, to the north of Perth. Young Beatrix had her interest and imagination fired by a rich and varied wildlife as well as those tales of enchantment told by Miss McKenzie.

The wooded area was populated by deer and she would hear the gruff alarm call of roebuck. Summertime was the season when the does dropped their offspring – and, mated, began to nurture another generation of these shy woodlanders. The implantation was delayed until November; the roe kids appeared in spring, when there was a bounty of fresh food.

For Beatrix, rabbits were a favourite subject for investigation and art. Dead rabbits were skinned and their anatomy studied and drawn. On the other hand, a tame rabbit that was fussed over subsequently became a celebrated literary figure – Peter Rabbit. Beatrix plucked specimens of flowers and spent hours painting them in delicate watercolours.

In 1893 Beatrix's lifelong obsession, writing and portraying the aforementioned little animals – furred and feathered, who wore human clothes and had human traits - had an innocuous beginning. She searched for something to write about to cheer up Noel Moore, the ailing five-year-old son of a favourite governess and decided, instead of the customary get-well letter, to pen him a story about four rabbits, named: Flopsy, Mopsy, Cottontail and Peter.

When Dalguise House was no longer available, the Potters found holiday accommodation in Lakeland. It was to be a favoured holiday region for twenty-one years. The first property to claim their attention, for 1882 only, was Wray Castle, a stern, pseudo-baronial mansion on the west shore of Windermere. It had been recommended to the Potters by John Bright, MP, an old friend of Rupert.

This castle was a chilling sham, constructed in 1848 on the instructions of Dr Dawson, a wine-shipper from Liverpool who lived in a cottage until a storm dislodged a slate. Dawson vowed to build a house that would withstand the weather. Stone for Wray Castle, quarried on the eastern side of Windermere, was conveyed by boat to near the site and,

The Potters had long holidays in the heart of Lakeland, epitomised by this view of the Langdale Pikes.

Wray Castle, which the Potters rented for a Lakeland holiday.

according to Beatrix's chatty journal - encoded long after her death - was dragged up to the site of the house "on a kind of tram way". Dawson, a widower for many years, lived alone right up to his death at the age of ninety-six.

Wray Castle had little basic appeal for the Potters. Rupert took photographs of the building's stern exterior. Beatrix (aged 16) sketched and made watercolour paintings of whatever took her fancy. The brightest memory for the Potters was the visit paid to them by the local vicar, Rev Hardwicke Rawnsley, a stocky, bearded man of energy, charm and erudition. Through him, Beatrix became conscious of the natural beauty of the Lake District. He encouraged her to publish some of her work. He was one of the founders of The National Trust.

In 1906, Rawnsley penned his book *Months at the Lakes*. The chapter dealing with August gives us a hint of what the Potters might have experienced during their holiday at Wray. Beatrix was ultra-sensitive to weather and wildlife. Rawnsley first dealt with the weather, which in August "has an unfortunate way of beginning with fair promise at dawn and breaking her promises about two o'clock in the afternoon...the dolorous sadness of the afternoon is forgotten in the glory and joy of the eventide."

Rawnsley enthused about the flowering of the heather on the hills. He exulted at seeing Grass of Parnassus. Yet, seeing it, he was sad, "knowing that with it has come the ending of the flower time of the year." The birds of August were the martins and swallows. Young broods were on the wing. The cheery starling "perches on the chimney top or on the cottage roof-ridge" and "runs through his ventriloquist tricks each dawn..."

Over:
Left: Rydal Water and Nab Cottage.
Right: Whitewashed farmhouse in Great Langdale.

A comparative slack season on Lakeland farms in August made it possible for holiday folk to be welcomed. The fashion of "tekking in parties" grew rapidly. A few years ago, if you had asked a farmer's wife if she let her rooms, she would reply that she couldn't be bothered. At the present time, Rawnsley observed, "there was hardly a farm in the dales that will not open its doors ...The woman-body at a Lakeland farm is 't'maister', and rightly – there is not a shrewder or more capable race of farm wives in Britain – and she has come to look upon the farm guest as her particular perquisite."

The Potters summered at Lingholm and Fawe Park, two large estates on the western shore of Derwentwater. Lingholm, which the Potters rented for nine holidays, yielded the idea and treatment of *The Tale of Squirrel Nutkin*, this being based on a lake (Derwentwater), on a fell (Catbells) and on a grand little valley (Newlands). In her imagination St Herbert's Island became Owl Island and some squirrels were given the status of islanders. She portrayed them crossing the lake on rafts, using their upturned tails as sails! Mrs Tiggy Winkle, the washerwoman hedgehog, lived back o' Catbells.

The Potters stayed at Holehird, a mansion above Windermere, and Beatrix was thrilled by a pastoral landscape backed by mountains (known in the Lake District as fells). In 1896, the Potters prospected for furnished property in the Southern Lakes. Rupert, Helen and Beatrix stayed at the *Ferry Hotel*, on the Lancashire side of Windermere and close to where the ferry grounded.

Their choice that year was Sawrey. The family, including son Bertram, travelled northwards from London with coach, horses and servants. They settled at Lakefield, an imposing house overlooking Esthwaite Water which became known as Ees Wyke, meaning "house on the shore". Rupert, keen angler, was within easy distance of the lake. The appeal for Helen and Beatrix was mainly in the picturesque landscape.

They stayed here for three months. Rain fell steadily but did not discourage Beatrix from driving herself around the area by horse and trap and in the company of Don, a wiry collie. She undertook a fungus foray and, in contrast, at Hawkshead, she watched – doubtless open-

**Lakefield, Sawrey, which the Potters rented
for a holiday in the summer of 1896.**

Windermere from Lingmoor.
Opposite: St Mary's Church at Ambleside.

mouthed – the arrival of Bostock and Wombwell's Menagerie. Their vans were being hauled by elephants and camels!

During the Potter family's long summer holiday at Sawrey, some of the servants lodged at Hill Top. Enchanted by this old farmstead, Beatrix bought it, explaining to her parents that it was an investment. Money received as royalties on the sale of her books and a small legacy from an aunt covered the cost of this unpretentious building, with its flagged ground floor, its funny old fireplace, and creaky stairs. It had a delightful whiff of antiquity. And of freedom, for in due course Beatrix would regard it as home. After all, she had lived with her parents until she was almost forty.

ST. MARY'S PARISH CHU
SUNDAY SERVICES
HOLY COMMUNION 8.00
PARISH COMMUNION 10.4
EVENSONG 6.00
SEE PORCH NOTICEBOARD FOR
VICAR: THE REVEREND I.G. HIGDON
VISITORS ARE ALWAYS WELC

St Mary's Parish Church
CAR ACCESS FOR
CHURCH ONLY
NO CYCLING
ON LEAD

PLEASE DO NOT
LET YOUR DOG
FOUL THE
CHURCHYARD

**A gate at Sawrey which Beatrix incorporated into one of her paintings.
Opposite: Mrs Chapman of Sawrey, a bearded lady.**

She was not in the best of health, grieving over the death of Norman
Warne, one of three brothers connected with the publishing house of
Warne who had a special responsibility for her little books. Beatrix and
Norman had been engaged for a short time before she joined her family
on a holiday in Lakeland. He died unexpectedly, a long way off. This
being autumn, when Lakeland donned its cloak of tinted leaves, and
there was melancholia in the landscape, it must have been an effort for
Beatrix to smile.

Hill Top, Sawrey – Beatrix's first Lakeland home. (photo courtesy National Trust)

3: A Hilltop Home

Beatrix, this offcomer from London, bought Hill Top in 1905. With the farm came John Cannon, tenant farmer, and a small flock of sheep of the local Herdwick breed. Beatrix had the house extended to provide a parlour with bedrooms above for the farmer and his family. In the part of the house she retained for her use, Beatrix slept in a big brass-headed bed.

For eight years, until her marriage, she lived at the family home in London, using Hill Top as her holiday accommodation and a repository for her most prized antique furniture. She was charmed with the place, inside and out, as water-colour illustrations in some of her little books testify. John's new role was that of cowman, foreman and shepherd. His wife, housekeeper-cum-dairywoman, cared for Beatrix when she stayed here at Easter, when her father – who was in poor health - headed further south.

I lost no time in knocking on the door of Hill Top, which had become the property of The National Trust. The door was opened by Freda Jackson, a daughter of Tom Storey. She gave me a brief glimpse of the rooms and their contents, apologising for the untidiness and dust. Alterations had been carried out; the workmen were not long departed. I had my first viewing of Delmar Banner's celebrated painting of Beatrix, set against the showfield at Keswick. In the picture was a lady with a round, cherubic face, wearing homespun clothes, and holding an umbrella which, I was told, had belonged to Norman Warne, her one true love.

Beatrix's life became closely associated with the house. As I wandered round I half expected to find her busy at her needlework or thumbing over the certificates she had won at local shows with her Herdwick sheep. In view were miniatures of the characters she had created. Just as Squirrel Nutkin collected nuts in the autumn, so Beatrix – squirrel-like – gathered round herself a stock of quaint but beautiful objects. She retained the main part of Hill Top for her own use. The old flagged kitchen became an entrance hall.

Beatrix outside Hill Top in 1913. (photo courtesy National Trust)

In the year following Beatrix's death, the house had become, in a sense, a museum. Among the thousands of visitors was an Australian lady. She sat looking at the window ledge for a long time, then remarked: "Isn't it wonderful. They've even kept her vacuum flask." The flask was, indeed, used by Susan Ludbrook, the first curator. A sudden influx of visitors had left her no time to conceal it.

Hill Top Farm fulfilled all Beatrix's longings for roots and a home. Farmers were annoyed when she bought land that normally would have been taken over by neighbours. After her marriage, in 1913, Beatrix, indifferent to their grumbling, continued to make practical use of information given to her, on the quiet, by Willie Heelis, her solicitor husband, who had his fingers firmly on the pulse of local life. They were living at secluded Castle Cottage. Beatrix gave the impression, by welcoming visitors at Hill Top, that this was her main residence.

She was now in her twilight years as a writer but astute enough to draw on local instances for her animal tales. Rabbits were kept in a hutch in the garden and visiting children came to regard them as "relations" of Peter Rabbit. The hutch was of the bottomless type that could be moved daily to enable the animals to have fresh grass to nibble.

With advice and help from John Cannon, Beatrix attuned herself to local farming. She had a sheepdog called Kep. Her first experience was with pigs. Tom was known in the district for his skill at "butching" them. She lost interest in them when, disappointingly, there was a litter that did not thrive. Tom Storey used to "butch" at Hill Top, explaining: "She had a licensed slaughter-house. At t'back end time of year, she arranged for lambs to be butched and the meat taken round the village. Meat was cheap in those days. Dressed lamb brought about sixpence a pound."

Freda Jackson, who had grown up in Sawrey, mentioned Beatrix's regard for animals. This extended to guinea pigs and white mice. According to Freda, Beatrix never attended church at Sawrey, journeying in her old-fashioned car – chauffeur, the faithful Walter Stevens - to the church at Troutbeck. At the same time she would visit her mother, who lived at Lindeth Howe. Harry Byers, Beatrix's gardener at her new home, Castle Cottage, also tended the garden at Hill Top.

Tom Storey, third from right, at a gathering of flockmasters.

He, his wife Ethel and daughter lived at Fair Rigg, beside Ferry Hill. A much-respected man locally, he was for forty years a warden at Sawrey church.

Beatrix abhored modernity. She would not permit electricity to be installed at Hill Top, though she allowed the shippon to be wired up. The cows might like it! She was the last person in the village to get "t'lectric" and that was a year or two after its local introduction and when an electricity cable ran beside her house.

Whenever I was in the Sawrey area, I'd pop in to see Tom Storey for what Lakeland folk call a *crack* [gossip]. Tom was a typical Lakeland dalesman – small, spare, quiet-spoken, with a wry sense of humour. He respected his famous employer but was not above having a dig at her when she said or did something which in a farming sense was – daft. Tom's later years were spent in a lile cottage at the end of a row at Near Sawrey. I'd first see him through the window. He'd be sitting in a fireside

Elterwater village, at the entrance to Great Langdale.

chair, in an uncluttered room. He'd wave. I'd enter to a warm welcome – and often a nip o' summat strong.

Tom, who worked for Beatrix for many years, was a Barrovian. He explained his wheeziness to me by saying he was pigeon-chested. It was for this reason he had flitted from town to the cleaner air of the Lake District. Tom and his family had moved to Sawrey from Troutbeck Farm, piling their belongings on the back of a motor lorry kept by Beatrix for heavy farm jobs. Tom was most happy when he was in the company of fell farmers, as at shows and when some of them gathered to "leuk sheep".

Hill Top Farm consisted of almost 200 acres, forty of which were meadow, mown each summer using a double-horse machine and converted by wind and sun into hay - winter fodder for the stock. At Sawrey, haytime men did not go short of food or drink. Beatrix bought the customary barrel of ale.

Before the Storeys arrived, Beatrix hired a dairymaid. Now a milk separator was available; the cream was converted into butter or cheese. Shorthorns, still the most common type of cow, were milked by hand, the milker sitting on a three-legged stool, the jets of milk squirting noisily against the sides of a bucket. The milker tried to avoid the swish of the cow tail, to which pieces of hardened dung clung. Known as muck-buttons, they might cause nasty scars on the milker's face.

One lambing time, Beatrix had an unusual request. She said to Tom: "When the next lamb dies, take its head off, skin it back to the shoulders and let me have the head." Tom obliged and recalled that "she fastened it against a wall and sat on a copy [stool] in the field, painting it." Beatrix still spent part of her time writing. When Tom and his family were settled at Hill Top, she produced *The Fairy Caravan*. Tom got the first copy. "I have it in there now. It had that much handling, it had to have a new back put on."

Tom summed up Beatrix in a broadcast on Radio Cumbria. She was "rather quiet, reserved, but good to work for if you went the right way about it…She was a good farmer. She took notice of her men…She'd never done any farming. She learnt as she went on from her farm men and local farmers. When it was suggested that she looked rather like Mrs Tiggywinkle, the hedgehog, featured in one of her books, Tom replied: "Aye – she was rather stooped."

A real-life Peter Rabbit and many friends swarmed in a wood near Hill Top that belonged to the next estate. The rabbits ventured out to graze on her land, an area known as The Heights. Something must be done about it! Willie Heelis and Captain Duke went out with a net, rigged it up near the wood, left the net furled until the rabbits had passed, then slipped the netting down in the hope of capturing rabbits as they sped for cover.

It was a good idea which was not a great success in practice. Tom said: "They were cute, were rabbits, you know." Beatrix could also be cute. A field that lay half way up Ferry Hill was sold to her with the proviso that she would provide a seat on which people might rest and admire a view of Windermere. Beatrix did not provide a seat, considering that the idea smacked too much of tourism.

4: Courtship and Marriage

Beatrix became engaged to Norman Warne at the age of thirty-nine. Norman was, as aforementioned, the youngest of three brothers in the publishing house that was greatly profiting from her books. To her parents he was "trade" and thus socially beneath them. Romance won in the end and they were engaged. Norman slipped a gold ring over the appropriate finger. Beatrix's surge of joy changed to grief a fortnight later. He died of pernicious anaemia.

Years later, the engagement ring was lost – then, happily, found - in a hayfield at Hill Top, Sawrey. Beatrix had, by her own confession, been very naughty, tossing hay when forbidden such frolics by the doctor. "Then my belt support slipped off, and down I fell! I felt such a fool – they had to carry me in." When, in later life, she attended outdoor events such as sheep shows, Beatrix invariably carried a reminder of her first, brief romance – an umbrella that had belonged to Norman Warne.

Beatrix bought Castle Farm in the summer of 1909. Deciding to live here, with Hill Top in view, she named it Castle Cottage. The modest acreages abutted that of Hill Top. The two places were connected by footpath. Naturally, W H Heelis and Son had arranged the purchase. Beatrix, commuting from Bolton Gardens, the family's London home, to northernmost Lancashire, grew to rely on Willie Heelis's reports (when absent from Sawley) and his informative company (on her return).

His first meeting with Beatrix had been on one of her visits to Lakeland from the family home in London. She sought his legal advice. Having the means to buy property, a professional was needed to attend to her affairs. Willie and Beatrix occasionally visited Lakeland properties that she might, at a sale, add to her growing list.

Willie came from a notable north-country family, traceable to the Craven district of Yorkshire, where in 1652 a yeoman named John Heelis, of Addingham, was given a 99-year lease on land at Skibeden by Lady Anne Clifford. He married a Moorhouse from Skipton and a

Castle Cottage, Sawrey. Beatrix had a bow window fitted.

descendant named Thomas became agent to the Earl of Thanet at Skipton Castle and subsequently at Appleby Castle. In Willie's distinguished family were clerics, doctors, land agents and solicitors. Edward Heelis, his grandfather, had the Rectorship of Long Marton, in the Eden Valley, for over forty years. He married Esther, a member of the Martin family of Patterdale. She bore him eleven children.

Willie was one of four brothers. Two, like him, became solicitors; the other two went into Church service. Willie's career had begun in 1899 with an old-established firm of solicitors at Hawkshead. He lodged with his two spinster sisters at Hawkshead Hall. Having family links with the Eden Valley, he became widely known as Appleby Bill.

During the courtship period, Willie arrived at Sawrey on his fashionable Bradbury motor bike with a wickerwork sidecar. A local man pointed

The business premises at Hawkshead of William Heelis.

out to me the wall behind which the outfit was parked and where Willie made himself presentable before joining Beatrix for an evening's courting. Just before the engagement was announced, the wife of Willie's partner in the solicitors' practice met Beatrix in Kendal. She must have blinked at least twice at the sight of her be-shawled, tweed-swaddled figure, clattering along in clogs and carrying a butter basket containing flowers.

Willie eventually proposed marriage. It was, in effect, a proposal to continue, at an official level, the continuation of a deep friendship. There was the usual objection from her parents, who – in poor health, as indeed was Beatrix – pointed out a decided difference in social status between Willie and Beatrix. Yawn, yawn. They agreed to the marriage when their only son, Bertram, arriving unexpectedly from Scotland, dropped the proverbial bombshell. He had been secretly married for eleven years. The upturn for Beatrix began in the spring of 1913 with a grudging permission to consider herself engaged. Coincidentally, she experienced an improvement in health.

Willie was reportedly gaunt, handsome, of moderate height, unsmiling, taciturn – colourless, indeed. Annie Black – the lady who had first recalled Beatrix Potter to me – said he was "real north-country". He was happy-go-lucky, equally fond of business and pleasure.

Shortly before her marriage to Willie Heelis, a large room was built on the side of Castle Cottage. Beatrix continued to find animals appealing. A tiny black girl-pig, which was not included in the sale of a litter of pigs, was picked up by Beatrix and taken into the house; it slept in a basket by the side of her bed. It was bottle-fed until capable of feeding itself.

Beatrix was shy of people, especially men. Yet the second phase of her life - the Lakeland phase of thirty years - began with her marriage to Willie Heelis in October, 1913. He was little known outside Lakeland, where he was quietly respected. In contrast, Beatrix Potter was world-famous through her score of little books and the spin-off from a wide range of products, from painting books and slippers to hot water bottles. When the happy couple had become engaged, and a formal studio photograph was taken, an ornate chair was the main prop. A tight-lipped Beatrix sat on the chair and Willie balanced himself on one of the chair arms.

They were married at St Mary Abbot's Church, Kensington, in the autumn of 1913. At 42 years of age, he was five years younger than Beatrix. Rupert and Helen Potter had the grace to attend the ceremony; they signed the register. A photograph taken that day shows the couple with expressionless faces and wearing the clothes worn for the engagement print. Their roles were reversed. It was Beatrix who stood. Perhaps this was to allow for her hat on which was a mass of artificial blossom. Willie, sitting self-consciously, had crossed both arms and legs.

They honeymooned in London. As they were about to drive home, they collected a calf, placing it on the back seat of their car. In Sawrey, according to Annie Black, "she went round the village with wedding cake and knife on a plate. As she served the cake to the villagers, she remarked: 'I'm not Beatrix Potter any more; I'm Mrs Heelis'."

The Westmorland Gazette reported: "In the quietest of quiet manners, two very well-known local inhabitants were married in London on Wednesday. The two parties to this most interesting wedding were Mr W Heelis of Hawkshead Hall and Miss Helen Beatrix Potter of Hill Top, Sawrey. None of their friends knew of the wedding, which was solemnized in the simplest form, characteristic of such modest though accomplished bridegroom and bride..."

They got on very well in married life; she never interfered with his comings-and-goings, though you never saw them much together. Tom Storey summed him up in one sentence: "He was quite a nice chap."

To Beatrix, privacy was something to be greatly valued. The newly-weds settled down in Castle Cottage rather than Hill Top, which was in part a farmhouse. Beatrix, not wanting people to think she had forsaken Hill Top altogether, quite often visited the property, almost always when she was having people to tea. This led them to believe that she and her husband still lived there.

Willow Taylor, who grew up at Near Sawrey in Beatrix's time.

Beatrix was now a full-time resident of Sawrey, the village she had known – and loved – since the Potters had rented the big house overlooking Esthwaite Water for a holiday stay. To Beatrix, the folk of Sawrey were "such nice old-fashioned people...It is as nearly perfect a little place as I ever lived in." She liked its setting - "very pretty hill country, but not wild like Keswick or Ullswater." A Unitarian, Beatrix had no spiritual allegiance to the parish church. What suited her best was the Quaker Meeting House at Colthouse. She attended occasionally.

Tom Storey told me that Willie did a lot for the farming community. He gave helpful advice even on Saturdays if the farmers called at his house and asked for it." When he invested in a car, his progress from Sawrey to the office at Hawkshead could be followed. He grated his gears at every corner. Beatrix occasionally visited London to attend to her ailing father. Willie, in his turn, visited an ailing aunt living at Appleby.

Beatrix was being pestered by her publishers, who wanted another book. At Christmas, Beatrix and Willie joined the Heelis aunties and visiting members of the clan at Battlebarrow House, Appleby. Beatrix's contribution to the meal was a Hawkshead Cake of raisin-speckled pasty, the second cousin of an Eccles Cake.

Married life for the not-so-young couple was convivial, though they did not get under each other's feet. Annie summed him up as a happy-go-lucky man who was fond of business and of pleasure, which included country dancing." Like the other male dancers, he sported white flannels and had an open-neck shirt. Clara Boyle, of Eller How, Ambleside, who provided me with many biographical sketches of prominent Lakelanders for *Cumbria* magazine, knew Willie Heelis well.

Cumberland and Westmorland style wrestler in traditional garb.

As a solicitor he dealt with affairs relating to the Boyle family; he had also officiated as the solicitor for Beatrix. He was tall and broad, more likely to be taken for a farmer than a professional man. A lover of the simple life, he was gentle and gifted with an understanding smile. He had a quiet, unruffled voice. When Willie Heelis was approaching the canonical age, and somewhat deaf, he was still devoted to folk dancing. Clara had his support as she attempted to revive dancing in the locality. Willie regularly attended weekly gatherings she organised in Sawrey and at Hawkshead.

Beatrix, who always accompanied him, never danced a step. Being stumpy and bent, Beatrix gave the impression that dancing would to her induce pain. While Willie, like the other men, sported white flannels and open-neck shirt, she sat in her rough, dark tweed skirt that was pinned up behind with a large safety pin. A tight-fitting bodice was buttoned up in front. She always looked out of place on such festive occasions – unless, wrote Clara, you observed her sweet smile and the loving eyes with which she followed every move of her Willie. Those eyes "lit up with the lamp of comradeship and devotion."

Willie was fond of many other forms of sport – shooting, bowls and billiards. Yet folk dancing was the premier interest. Ethel Byers, one of the Sawrey team who was driven to a dancing event by Willie Heelis, recalled that four of the passengers sat in a "dicky" seat at the back of the car. It was a foggy night. Willie, who was not a good driver at the

William Heelis with folk dancers, early 1930s.

Folk dancers in Langdale.

best of times, followed the tail-lights of one or two vehicles – and eventually braked the car in a cul-de-sac. It was someone's private drive.

The great event in Willie Heelis's career as a folk dancer came when, in 1930, a large annual festival gathering took place at Underley Hall, by kind invitation of Lord and Lady Henry Cavendish Bentinck. About one thousand dancers were observed by an equally large number of spectators. Willie danced his *Newcastle* and *Old Mole* with the best, a great credit to the Sawrey team.

Then (Clara recalled) came the great moment when the three oldest men dancers of the Lake District – Mr Brady, the 70-year-old little postmaster of Sedgwick, still an ardent rock-climber; Kenneth Spence, of Sawrey House, and Mr Heelis danced by themselves the old *Greensleeves* morris jig which, in its buffoonery, demands an appreciable amount of agility, sense of rhythm and of fun. The three elderly men acquitted themselves with honour, in spite of their having had only one real practice together. Clara noticed that Beatrix was radiant with pride. Her contribution was making dresses for the lady dancers. Sometimes there was dancing in the big kitchen at Hill Top.

Angling was another sporting favourite. Moss Eccles Tarn, half of which belonged to Beatrix, had been stocked with brown trout, which fed well in five acres of nutrient-rich water. On fishing trips, the oars were in the hands of Beatrix or Tom Storey. Their work was not so much rowing as keeping the heavy, flat-bottomed boat moving. Willie caught many fine fish, some of which he gave to Tom. His family did not care a big lot for them; they tasted "mossy".

There was a romantic ending to one angling expedition – a warm June night in 1924. Beatrix and Willie walked slowly homewards at the especially late hour of 11 pm. Another romantic touch was observed by the Banners when visiting Beatrix at Castle Cottage. When it was close to supper-time, Beatrix said: "Wait and see Willie". They waited quietly. She laid the table and put the silver candlesticks on it and lit the candles. "We felt we had been forgotten. She was looking forward to welcoming him home...It was romantic."

5: *Life at Castle Cottage*

The kitchen at Castle Cottage, as recalled by Amanda Postlethwaite, who lived nearby, had bare flags, a scrubbed table and ordinary ladderback chairs. Everything was kept beautiful and clean. You went out of the kitchen and down a passage into what was called the lounge. "I don't think it had a carpet all over, just in the middle, as people did in those days." In the lounge was a piano, a settee and some easy chairs. One or two little tables stood about. "She had a kind of veranda out of her lounge. It looked on to the garden. A big bedroom had bay windows..."

Tom Storey told me about the flagged floors, adding that Mrs Heelis – as he respectfully knew her - was always up and about in good time. "Wherever she was, you'd hear the clatter of her clogs." Beatrix and Willie, working amicably together, were assisted in cooking and housework by Mrs Benson and Mrs Rogerson, widows who had cottages in the village. Tommy Christie attended to the garden. A small orchard at the back of the house looked after itself.

Every morning, Tom Storey took the milk to Castle Cottage. "Mrs Heelis sometimes had two pints, but more often just one pint...She used to meet me at the door". She did not work on the farm. "You might see her in the hayfield with a fork, doing a little bit of haymaking, but that was all...You'd see her walking round the fields, and if she knew you had show-sheep in t'yard she'd walk round to look at them. I'd tell her when anything special was happening."

Josephina Banner, who met Beatrix in her home, said: "She was radiant and jolly. She had silvery-white hair, very rosy cheeks, blue eyes, and a lovely smile. Very round and fat, when laughing she would rock backwards and forwards on her chair and slap her little knees. Josephina acknowledged that "if she was that side out, she had no room

Mr Postlethwaite, photographed by Beatrix. Two children are pictured!

Joephina, sculptress wife of the artist Delmar Banner.

for children." Yet "children loved her through her books; they met her there."

Her appearance during the Lakeland years was a talking point for both locals and visitors. She did not dress up especially well. When attending Hawkshead Show, she made an effort – but her best clothes were old. She didn't care about dress. And did not care much for those who did. The black clogs, with clasps to fasten them, were made by Charlie Brown, of Hawkshead, who used *kip* or split leather, beech soles and iron caulkers or "irons". Beatrix had rather small feet. She didn't take above size four.

During her marriage, the considerable artistic powers that produced a run of classic children's books were on the wane. Beatrix now used much of her wit and energy in farming. She was shifting from paper-book animals to real animals. She was also keen to buy up property threatened by modern development. Her energies and money were dedicated to the well-being of old buildings, old ways.

To discover what life had been like at Castle Cottage, in the 1930s, I visited two of her close friends, Josephina and Delmar Banner, at *The Bield*, their 300-year-old farmstead in Little Langdale. As related, Josephina was introduced to Beatrix at an Eskdale Show. Josephina was born near London, the daughter of a Brazilian father and a mother of English Quaker stock who had associations with Maryport. She acquired sculptural skills in the yards of stone masons, at the Regent Street Polytechnic, the Royal Academy Schools and through studies in

Florence, Paris and Rio. She met the man who would become her husband during student days.

Delmar became an outstanding painter, with a fondness for mountaintops – sculpted rocks and the elusive misty air that gathered round them. He observed: "It is the supreme character of the fells, as the eye tries to grasp them that they are objects of solid granite, fire-tempered, ice-hewn and enduring through a long time. Yet also they are distant, mysterious, swimming in a sea of air and light and colour that shifts and dissolves and obscures."

The Banners had lived among the dalehead families for years before settling down at *The Bield*. I noticed a frieze round one of the rooms and was informed that it was painted by Delmar entirely from drawings made during seven hours spent on the summit of Glaramara. He had mixed petroleum with oil paint to get the desired matt finish.

Delmar cheerfully ignored the weather, sharing a view expressed by Heaton Cooper, that there was no good or bad day in the Lake District; it was either wet or dry. For his mountain paintings, drawings and notes were made out of doors; he made sketches in pencil. "His pencil walked the tops," said Josephina. At times, he sketched in colour. The actual painting at *The Bield* was carried out in what had formerly been a bracken loft. It was a chancy occupation; he did not make a living from art. As Josephina remarked: "No one did unless they were paid for teaching art or had a private income."

Josephina got to know Beatrix through Cyril Bulman; they were introduced by him at Eskdale Show. "She took a very quiet look at me." Beatrix had then said, in a flat but well modulated voice: "You can come and see me one day." A date was given. The Banners went. After several meetings, Beatrix bought two of Delmar's watercolours. Josephina, when asked about them, could not remember what happened to them. "One painting was of a fox hiding in the snow." What had attracted Beatrix to the picture was that it was "in a style you'll never do again." She would keep it as a record. Josephina said of Beatrix: "She had great character. Everything she did followed her own ways."

National Trust farm in Little Langdale – a valley that was home to the artistic Banners.

I asked about Delmar's technique for his celebrated portrait of Beatrix on a Lakeland showfield – a picture that hangs in Hill Top, with a copy in the National Portrait Gallery. Delmar used his imagination based on experience of the subject. Said Josephina: "We both have visual memories. It's like 'perfect tone' in music." Beatrix had not posed for the portrait. Delmar was not the type of artist who had a subject before him which he copied. The restless Beatrix would not have conformed!

Josephina and Delmar, like Beatrix, were entranced by local customs. Josephina mentioned a Norse-type custom relating to *arvel bread* – a type of bread eaten after someone had died. Those who arrived at the house door, on their way to view the corpse, took a piece of the special bread from a basket held by a young man. You ate it and then went in." At my last meeting with Josephina, when she was old, wizened but mentally adroit, occupying a living room-cum-bedroom off Stricklandgate in Kendal, she told me about the Sin-Eater. "There was a corpse in a coffin that rested on two sheep-shearing benches in front of the fire. The family of the deceased had gathered round, leaving the centre of the room empty. The front door of the house was left open. After sunset, the Sin-eater emerged from the darkness and entered the house. On the chest of the corpse was a pile of salt. The Sin-eater walked up to the body, took a handful of salt, swallowed it, then walked back into the night. In doing that he had eaten the sins of the man."

 What did Delmar think of Beatrix? She was "a snug woman – shrewd and solid and realistic, like her paintings." Josephina was enchanted by Beatrix in her setting of Castle Cottage. "She was tiny, and the older she got the tinier and rounder she became. And she was so cute and pretty – the prettiest old lady I have ever met. The eyes were of a brilliant blue. She had lovely rosy cheeks and soft white hair, done up at the top with a little black velvet bow." (Few people knew that a girlhood attack of rheumatic fever had left Beatrix with a gap in her hair that she did her best to conceal).

Beatrix's eyesight had deteriorated; she no longer had keen enough sight to enable her to paint delicate watercolours. Cherishing her original paintings, each measuring about 12 by 8 inches, she had wrapped them in brown paper with a blue ribbon and kept behind the geyser in the bathroom. Josephina commented: "Even in this matter, she was completely original."

Visiting Castle Cottage for the first time, the Banners had to go through the gardens of two other houses to reach it. (They later became familiar with a door that gave access to a back lane). On that first visit, Josephina had drawn attention to their presence by rapping her knuckles on the small green door, there being no knocker to use. "There was a long silence. Then Delmar and I heard little clogs toddling along on the flags beyond the door. They toddled up to the door. Then they stopped. We felt it was just like a little mouse, stopping to sniff the air, to try and detect who was coming. Then gradually she opened the door until it was two or three inches wide.

"We saw her little face peep through. She recognised us. She opened the door a little and said: 'Coom in'. And do you know what she was wearing on her head? One of those old-fashioned tea-cosies which are knitted and have a hole for the spout." It was a blue tea-cosy. "She looked so cute, like one of her dressed-up little animals."

Beatrix did not shake hands with her visitors. "She turned and toddled off. We just followed her. Delmar shut the door behind us. We found ourselves in a flagged hall. There was no mat. Two beautiful old guns, with silver mountings, adorned a beam. Then, on the right, there was a door into this lovely old room". It was not over-furnished. "There was a fireplace with two easy chairs, comfortable in Victorian red velvet. I remember an old-fashioned dining table. We saw some chocolate wrappers – what Delmar later declared was a naughty amount of chocolate paper."

Some straight-backed chairs were available. The visitors sat on these. "We sat there, rather politely, because Beatrix was very awe-inspiring as well as being sweetly pretty - like the little dog Duchess!" She began to ask questions. "As we answered, and she discovered that we knew the Lakes, and a number of local farmers, intimately, she began to open up and became very friendly.

"She said something very funny: I laughed, and as I laughed I snorted. My husband said: 'Oh. Pig-wig!' a nickname that made Beatrix laugh. She opened her brilliant blue eyes very wide, stopped and looked from one to the other, then said: Do you call him Pigwig?" After this, it amused her to do so; she very often used the name Pigwig when she wrote to me." Josephina had such clear recollections of that first visit to Castle Cottage she could recall fine details of a Girton that hung there. "It was so suitable – a shepherd and sheep running for shelter from an approaching storm."

Amanda told me about a pre-Christmas party for the children of Sawrey; it was held on a Saturday afternoon, from 3 pm until 6 pm. Beatrix opened up her sitting room, having all the things taken to other parts of the house. "We always started with tea, served in a big room upstairs." Mrs Rogerson made Christmas cake, jelly and other party food. "After this, we'd come downstairs and dance. Mr Heelis played

Mrs Postlethwaite and daughter. Beatrix and Mr Postlethwaite often chatted in the porch.

the pianola. He always started with a folk dance, *Roger de Coverley*. We children were aged from about five to ten. There'd be thirty of us. Mrs Heelis dressed herself up in her black satin and she was the life and soul of the party."

Beatrix was not a churchy person but, at Christmas she did become sentimental, keen to hear the church choir on its festive rounds of the village singing an unaccompanied hymn known as *The Sawrey Carol.*

Hark,
hark,
when news the angels bring;
glad tidings of a new-born King;
Born of a maiden virgin pure;
born without sin (bass singers),
born without sin from guilt secure (all).

The carollers were treated to minced pies and (for adults) mulled ale by the owners of the larger houses. In the pre-Christmas period of 1943, when Beatrix was very ill, having been in hospital in Liverpool), the carol singers were requested not to visit Castle Cottage.

Delmar and Josephina Banner, visiting the *Woolpack* in Eskdale, met a Professor of Agriculture at Durham. He recalled a meeting with Beatrix at Castle Cottage. As part of his studies into sheep diseases, he distributed a questionnaire in the district. One of the most helpful replies came from a farmer called B H Heelis. He made an appointment to see this farmer.

Arriving at Castle Cottage, he met "their little maid" who took him upstairs to a tiny room. In an enormous bed was this tiny, pretty old lady – B H Heelis, the farmer. He had tea with her and was enchanted by what she told him about sheep complaints. He found pleasure in her unique and delightful personality. Also in her unpretentious realism.

When she was writing, Beatrix might be taciturn for days on end. At other times she had the company of people who did not "live in" but had cottages in the village. The menu on such an occasion could be simple. A visitor for tea in the 1930s saw a green tablecloth with bobbles. Tea consisted of bread and butter, with no cake. Another visitor sat down to a plate of cold mutton. Only one half of the dining table had been cleared for the meal. The other half was cluttered with papers.

Conversely, when Josephina and Delmar Banner visited Beatrix, there was "plenty on the table and she herself had two helpings of everything." She did not dominate the conversation, being interested in all that Delmar had to say." Beatrix told Josephina that when she was off-colour, in bed, she looked through the window and saw there was just one cabbage left in the garden. It looked out of place. Beatrix kept on saying: "Pull up that cabbage." And nobody obliged. One day when nobody was about, Beatrix put on two pairs of knickers and her husband's raincoat. Going out, she tugged up the cabbage and then went happily back to bed.

Anthony Benson, shepherd, when visiting Castle Cottage en route from

one of her farms to his home at Troutbeck Farm, got no further than a chair just inside the kitchen. "That's where you sat, about two paces in. She'd fetch you a cup o' tea and a meat sandwich. And that was that!" With no lift offered, Anthony then had to trudge to the Windermere ferry, cross the lake, tramp to Bowness and on to Troutbeck. He added: "There wasn't a day lang enough."

Half closing his eyes, and giving his memory a gentle prodding, William H Waddington, a well-known Lakeland artist living at Windermere, told me of the years from 1916 when he saw Beatrix Potter almost every day. He and his wife, as her tenants, lived next door to her. Anyone approaching Castle Cottage passed along the bottom of their garden. So did Beatrix. A person of regular ways, she walked that way every morning at precisely the same time – followed by turkeys, ducks, geese and any other feathered creatures that happened to be near, for they knew that she had some hot mash in a bucket.

She stirred the mash with a stick, beating the bucket and singing a cadence of song. Mary Rogerson, the housekeeper at Castle Cottage, recalled when Beatrix's pet sow, named Sally, followed her around, sometimes even entering the dining room. Mercifully, the pig was house-trained. Tzusee and Chuleh, her dogs of the Pekingese breed, were trained to balance sugar lumps on their noses and also to perform a circular dance. Her Pomeranian was given the name Pom Ally.

The Waddingtons, who moved to Sawrey from Hawkshead Hill, had seen Beatrix on the recommendation of a friend knowing their need for fresh accommodation. She received them in a kindly way, remarking:

"I think I would rather like to have an artist living next door. He would not have a gramophone going in the garden…" She began to enumerate many other things that she did not believe a self-respecting artist would do and concluded: "I'm quite sure that you, as an artist, would agree with me."

Beatrix's mother, dumpy, clad in dark clothes, had affinities with Queen Victoria. Beatrix had settled her in a grand house at Storrs Park, on the Westmorland side of Windermere. The dutiful daughter, visiting her, trudged from Sawrey to the ferry, hoping that on the other shore her mother's carriage awaited her. Mrs Potter took a perverse pleasure in not sending it. When Beatrix arrived at mother's home, she was often ridiculed in front of the servants.

Mother visited Beatrix at Sawrey, travelling in a carriage and pair, with a coachman and flunkey in attendance. The Waddingtons watched the outfit being driven to Beatrix's home. When it returned, Beatrix herself would be sitting in it, wearing her old farming attire. This was in strong contrast with the garb of her mother. They would be driven to Bowness, where Beatrix would do her shopping. She would alight from the carriage and clatter across the causeway into the shops wearing the clogs she had worn in the farmyard before her mother collected her.

Although she looked like a farmer, her voice was cultured and refined. There was no trace of Westmorland dialect. I asked William Waddington what he thought of Beatrix's artistic work. He said: "It was extremely good. Her drawings were most sensitive and beautiful. She also showed very clever draughtmanship. Those illustrations were ideal for the purpose. She made careful studies of the animals; her drawings of them were anatomically perfect, being done from life."

What was Beatrix like as a landlord? "She could not have been kinder. She made me a big studio in the house by arranging for a wall to be knocked down. She went to considerable expense to make it a comfortable home."

6: Beloved Herdwicks

Initially, Beatrix thought there was something lovable about "the silly sheep and the simple old-fashioned talk of those who work the soil and the flock." The "silly sheep" became her beloved Herdwicks; the old-fashioned talk and quirky humour enthralled her. She had a coat and skirt made from Herdwick wool. On her way into the village, she met a farmer who – noticing her new suit – remarked: "You'd better not let tup see thi."

Beatrix's fascination with Herdwick sheep expressed itself in 1903 when, during a family holiday, she sketched the distinctive sheep marks on flocks around Fawe Park, Keswick. She was to write movingly of the death at Hill Top of a Herdwick ram, Saddleback Wedgewood, which belonged to Josiah Cockbain and was "a grand old champion of the fells...the perfect type of hard, big boned Herdwick tup, with strong clean legs, springy fetlocks, broad scope, fine horns, a grand jacket and mane."

The first Herdwicks she owned had been bought from Joseph Gregg. Joe, a native of Great Langdale, had been wounded during Army service in France during the 1914-18 war. He returned to Lakeland and resumed farming as tenant of Town End, Troutbeck. Joe's son, Vic, recalled: "My father and his brother, Noble Gregg, sold surplus sheep at Ambleside on a day when lambs were making from 3s.6d to 5s.6d." Beatrix was recalled as a quaint old lady wearing dark clothes who knew his father. "She'd give me a copper or two."

The Gregg family moved to Taw House, at the head of Eskdale, returning to Great Langdale in 1935. Beatrix had a hand in this move. Hearing from her husband it was available to let, and recalling Joe Gregg's kindness when she bought Troutbeck Park, she instructed her chauffeur to drive her to Taw House at a time when they were carting bracken for bedding. Said Vic: "To see a car coming into the yard of Taw House was something of a rarity."

They were having tea. "Mrs Heelis came to the door and said: 'Joe – I

Yew Tree Farm, Coniston

want a word with you.' They went through into the sitting room where she was offered the customary cup of tea and piece of cake. That night, father said: 'I'll not be here when you get up in the morning. You'll have to milk the cows and look after yourself. I'm going to Kendal.' He did not say what for.

"When he got back that night, he told us we would be moving to Millbeck in the spring. Mrs Heelis had made it possible by recommending him for the tenancy." Said Vic: "She was serious about the Herdwick sheep. If there was a sheep show, she'd be there – and wouldn't miss anything."

Herdwick sheep greeted strangers to the central fells, their high domain, with disdainful sneezing. A sheep of this breed occupied a plot of land where it was nurtured as a lamb. An old chap remarked: "Them sheep can live off next to nowt. When there's no sun to take t'chill out of t'grund, they mun eat lile bits o' briar and bits o' shoots."

Joe Relph of Threlkeld, told me: "We've a heavy rainfall in Lakeland. The Herdwick has been bred for generations to stand that rainfall. It has a coat and a waistcoat, a soft underjacket which is like thatching on a stack; it turns the rain wonderfully. What's more, it soon dries after heavy rain or soft snow. The snow doesn't stick to the fleece as it does with breeds that have a softer wool."

Joe switched his attention to the sheepdog. "We can't do without the collie...Even an Olympic champion couldn't hope to round up the sheep that roam over yon rough tawny ground." The older type of collie was employed in Lakeland. "It's been bred each side of the border for centuries. A hill collie must have a good wide run on the fell. It must not be scared of using itself. It has to give the sheep plenty of room; a dog that goes straight at them is no good at all."

Joe had eight dogs; he often took three or four with him when rounding up the sheep. How much ground would the average sheepdog cover in

Herdwick tups at Keswick Show.

Herdwicks and the Langdale Pikes.

a working day? Joe pondered on this for a while, then said it was a difficult question. "There are differences between dogs. Some collies will run all the time. Others tire and want a rest. But a dog that is always on the move might cover fifty miles of fell in a day."

We briefly touched on the relationship of sheep to dog. "Some people consider that sheep are not intelligent. My experience is that they are very clever. Sheep will quickly notice any weakness in the dog." He remembered the names of his dogs in threesomes and told me of some of the early animals he had owned – Tuss, Lady and Mack, Bright Jack, Kip and Fleet.

According to Tom and Anthony, her shepherds, Beatrix "didn't knaw a gurt lot about sheep. She was one o' those who'd take a fancy to one sheep when there were mebbe plenty o' better 'uns." At Keswick, where incidentally she was photographed with none other than Lady Leconfield, she talked her way to the sheep pens. "All the old sheep farmers knew Mrs Heelis. She'd talk for a week to a real old sheep farmer. On a thoroughly wet show-day, when the sheep looked draggled, she waterproofed herself, wearing a hessian bag on her head and shoulders and draping another from her waist."

At Keswick show, Tom Storey chatted with two friends. "We were leaning on the pens and straight across were our sheep." Beatrix walked down the side of the pens with Mr Mackereth, an old-time hind at Hill Top. "As it happened," Tom continued, "I was showing one sheep that she should have known. It was one of t'elder sheep, a ewe. I saw them walking near the pens, then stop suddenly. She talked about sheep. Then she whipped round and said: 'Which is such-and-such ewe, Storey, among these?' I said: 'Them aren't yours. Yours are in t'next pen'. Was her face red! I don't think she liked it but she daren't say anything. I was only telling the truth."

This wiry, goat-like type of sheep took its name from the *herdwyk* or sheep farm, such as was owned by the monks of Furness Abbey. Some folk claimed it was introduced by the Norsemen. More likely it was a native animal modified by nature and Lakeland flockmasters and by its cheerless environment. It is identifiable by its rimy face – hoar-frosted in appearance – and deep, round body. Strong white legs let it stand firm in a gale. The wool, when processed into cloth and left undyed, had become the celebrated John Peel's "coat so grey". The coat was not "so gay", as many suppose.

As mentioned, each Herdwick ewe formed a strong attachment to its heaf [natal area] from which it rarely moved. Stocks of sheep were inclined to intermingle at the edges. Herdwicks are weather-wise. A dalehead farmer told me: "It's the odd 'uns that are overblown. Nine times out of ten, the sheep'll come down the fell before they are likely to be caught by snow." It was known for an overblown Herdwick to use up what bit of herbage there was, then keep itself alive – nobbut just, as they said – by chewing its wool.

Beatrix was driven to the shows by her husband, the uncomplaining Willie, in his little Ford car. The first trophy she was awarded, at Hawkshead in 1928, was for a shearling. Two years later, her sheep claimed any number of major prizes at shows. Tom Storey received a cup marked Ennerdale, Loweswater, Eskdale, 1930, "for champion female." The cup had been made for Beatrix who, of course, retained the original trophy. She kept all the cups awarded for her sheep. Tom was allowed to retain teapots and tankards.

Tom Storey went with her to many of the fell shows, including Ennerdale, Loweswater, Gosforth and Eshd'l [Eskdale]. "If she lost, she didn't grumble. In her time, she won all the big prizes." Her favourite outfit was made of Herdwick tweed. "Once she gave me three fleeces from our show ewes and I had a suit made up from the wool. That suit was cut in the late thirties. It's rough tweed – but still (1980s) wears well."

In 1930, she became the first woman chairman of the Herdwick Sheep Breeders' Association, which had been established in 1899 by Hardwick Rawnsley, the cleric who was an old family friend. Beatrix judged at many of the local shows. Rawnsley was keen to preserve the Herdwick. Beatrix's passion for the breed was such that when a prize-winning ram called Wedgewood died, she sent an obituary to the *Westmorland Gazette*.

As she set out to attend one of the meetings of the Breeders' Association, she remarked: "I begin to look rather like an elderly sheep." It was whispered that in her spinsterhood she sometimes went to bed with a sheep in lieu of a warming-pan or stone bottle. This was untrue, though believable. The newly-wed Beatrix had taken a sick piglet into the conjugal bed for the night. (The piglet made a good recovery).

Beatrix was to be seen at markets, shows and shepherds' meets, revelling in old customs and appraising sheep. She was generally reserved and quiet. When she did speak – she spoke her mind! Tom worked for Beatrix for 18 years and was to serve under her husband for another two. My first chat with him took place in a turnip field when, at the invitation of his son, I clambered on to the back of a tractor-drawn trailer and was bumped and jostled up a steep, rocky lane to the field. Tom broke off turnip-pulling, straightened his back and told me about the gentle-eyed Miss Potter who became the bluff, forthright Mrs Heelis, champion sheep farmer.

Subsequent talks with Tom took place at his lile cottage at the end of a row at Near Sawrey. As already related, I'd first see him through the window. As mentioned, he'd be sitting in a fireside chair in an uncluttered room. He'd wave. I'd enter to a warm welcome – and sometimes a nip o' summat strong. Said Tom: "If she took to you - you were all right! She could be nasty with people she didn't like and she liked her own way about things." He got on well with her. Now and again, there was an interchange of angry words.

In 1963, I joined the Lakeland flockmasters round the pens at Eshd'l [Eskdale] Show, which was known as the Herdwick Royal. It was a time, remembered by Beatrix, when Herdwick tips [tups] were hired, not bought outright. This Show had a special appeal for her. In her day, the *Woolpack Inn* was the venue and afterwards "mine host" riddled the sand strewn on the floor before throwing it away. It might contain some lost sovereigns!

On the more recent occasion, I was enthralled by a conversation between fell farmers:

Whoo's ta gooing on today? Hesta any tips to part wid?
Well, I've yan or two.
This 'esn't mich coat on it.
It's reight enuff.
Whoo much ista wanting fer it?
Thirty bob.
Ah's going to gie thee twenty-five bob.
Split it.
Reight.

We were at Bridge End, Boot. The Show had brought flockmasters from all over Lakeland to talk about Herdwicks. A fell farmer told me some of the points to be taken into account when *kenning* a Herdwick tup. A good head was important. The face should be white and hairy and the nose broad. A "good and strong" back was vital. A sheep's woollen coat must be well suited to turning the storms. I gathered that horns were not all that important, though some "nice horns helps them a bit." A first prize card was handed to an aged tup that had only "bits o' stumps". It was a "cowed" ram. Tups that never develop horns were known locally as *cowies*.

I met farmers who remembered when sheep were walked here from all parts of the Lake District, some men spending three, four or more days away from home. Occasionally a man was out and about for a fortnight. "We started off travelling at about four

Tom Storey, Beatrix's shepherd at Near Sawrey.

Eskdale Show, where Beatrix was introduced to the Herdwick sheep breed. Opposite: Beatrix chatting with a visitor to Eskdale Show. (photo courtesy Victoria & Albert Museum)

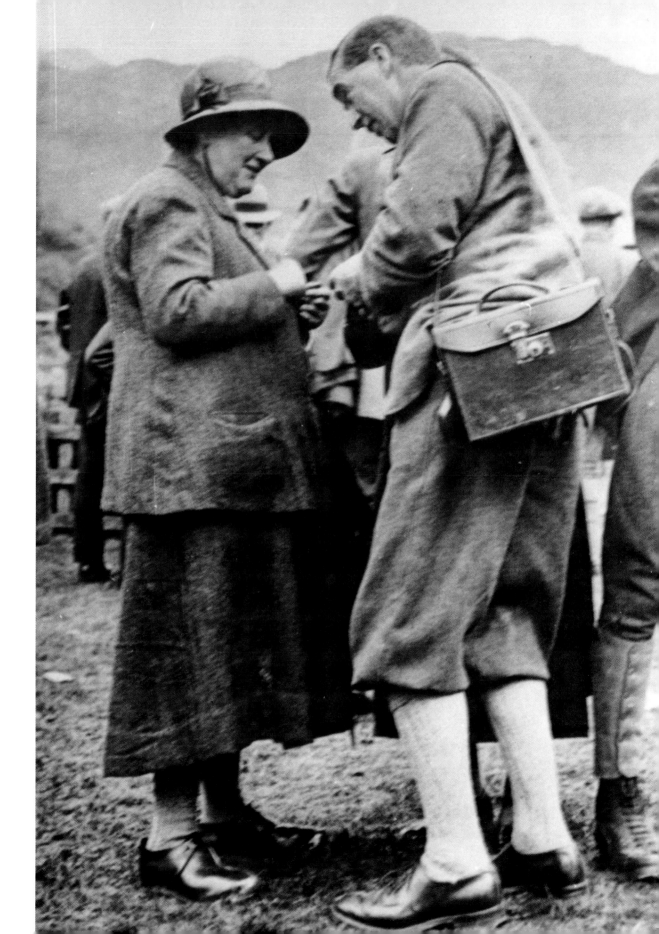

Herdwick ewes being rounded up at Tilberthwaite.

miles an hour, but it was down to one mile an hour towards the end," one veteran told me. I was astonished at the number of sheep that ground their teeth. A farmer to whom I inquired said: "It's just because they're standing idle in pens. They've nowt to do so they grind their teeth a bit."

Wasdale sheep came over Burnmoor. Those from Langdale used the great passes of Wrynose and Hardknott. Broughton stock was walked across Birker Moor. As I chatted with William Wilson, better known as Herdwick Billy, he recalled his days in Wasdale. On the morning of Eskdale Show he would be out of bed about 4.30 am to complete the farm jobs before driving stock across the moor. It was rare for him to be back at home on the same day. Joe Teasdale, of Caldbeck, brought a tup to Eskdale in a horse-drawn cart.

Business blended with pleasure to Eshd'l. Before the foot races were run, and the hound trails got under way; before, indeed, there were many visitors to the tents where produce and handicrafts were neatly arranged, judging and bargaining occurred round the pens of sheep. The process was never rushed. Pens were labelled with the names of farmers, not numbers, the commonplace at most events. Eshd'l, in fact, was a show held at the threshold of another farming year. Another event took place on the same site in May, when tups would be returned to their owners and monetary settlements for the hire were made.

In the early 1960s, a hire charge was usually between 25s and 30s. This curious situation developed to ensure a regular change of blood in a comparatively small and self-contained population of sheep. A Herdwick flockmaster raised tups that benefited the flocks of other men. "We like to see a bright-eyed sheep," said the tall, lean farmer who was clad in his best "setting off" suit and carried an ornate crook that had clearly never seen service on the fells.

He pointed out a good example of a tup. This animal was doing its best to break through into the next pen. What I witnessed was not a frenzy of heated destruction, but movements that were slow, thoughtful, systematic. The tup charged, the pen shook and creaked. The tup backed again and stood glaring at another tup beyond the barrier. A few minutes later, it charged again, and the wood splintered. More thought. Another charge. The wood gave way.

The tup allowed a slight expression of satisfaction to flicker across its hoary white face. It did not seem to be troubled by a headache. Said the farmer: "They stands up to some awful battles in t'mating season. They backs away and meets full smack with their heads. Sometimes they kill each other. Brokken necks, or feaster o' t'head when one's punctured an' t'germs git in."

At showtime, Beatrix saw men giving prize tups a rusty tinge. They broke open packets of reddish powder, diluted it with a light oil and applied the mixture to the coarse fleeces of their Herdwicks. The sole reason was to increase sheep's attractiveness. "It's just like when ladies daub themselves up. It improves t'look of 'em."

I noticed from the 1963 programme that the National Trust had offered a prize for one of the sheep classes, the emphasis being on "natural colour". The faces and legs of the Herdwicks were being washed with detergents or soap. I admired the strong, bony, well-lagged legs of the tups and was told that when a lad visited Eskdale from the country of the Swaledale sheep, he looked for a long time at a Herdwick tup and then said with wonderment: "Yon tewp's getten booits on."

Though genetically identical, there are noticeable differences between the tups that appear at the shows, commanding the keenest attention at hiring time, and those tups that remain on the fells, with little limelight. The best tups are specially fed or given improved grazings so that their full potential is brought out. Farmers watch the progress of these outstanding tups from the lamb stage right up to their time of greatest utility.

Many of those on view at the Eskdale Show were already "spoken for", being brought along to be picked up at this convenient place. Years before, some farmers made the rounds of farms where suitable tups were bred. This occurred on the Sunday before Eskdale Show and became known as Tup Sunday.

It was customary to hire a tup at Keswick in autumn and return it to its owner in the spring. At this fair, Beatrix wore the same old costume, day in and day out. "It was a thick tweed, stretching reet doon to her ankles." The old custom of hiring tups began to give way to outright sales. The best tups were in keen demand. If Mrs Heelis wanted one – she got it, paying £200 for an especially good animal.

To Josephina Banner, Beatrix was "the prettiest old lady I have ever met." She first encountered her at Eskdale Show. She was one of the judges. Paraded before the diminutive Beatrix were majestic Herdwicks, daubed with "show red". She was suitably attired in a tweedy outfit – browny green – with clogs on her feet and a felt hat, complete with elastic stretching under the chin to cheat any Lakeland breezes.

Josephina was introduced to Beatrix by Cyril and Sally Bulman, who had come to help their relations at the *Woolpack*, an old hostelry at Boot. Her husband Delmar was on the fells, sketching. Josephina recalled: "As a sculptor, I was wearing my usual working attire – boiler suit – and had clogs on my feet. I think she liked me instantly because of the clogs. We got on with each other because we were both straightforward people. The Banners watched her judging the stock. Then they saw her wander around the sheep section of the show, looking intently at animals in the pens. You could see that the farmers respected her."

Then a big, tall farmer approached her – and slapped her on the back, as he might have done with a well-built farmer friend. "The blow was so hard it nearly toppled her over, and she staggered. He had drunk too much and was just too friendly. He told her that his ancestors had known John Peel, the famous huntsman. Sometimes, when Peel was really drunk, one of the family had lifted him on to his horse. Beatrix was determined not to be impressed. She simply said: 'I've never thought owt of John Peel.' It was a brave thing to say in front of all those farmers, because they all thought that John Peel was marvellous."

Seeking more information about Herdwicks, in 1957 I chatted with William Wilson, who would have been known to Beatrix, though not

A gathering of Herdwick sheep,

Herdwick Billy, noted for his knowledge of the breed.

under that name. A workman in the fertile Derwent Valley whom I approached for details of the flockmaster's home straightened his back and rested an elbow on the handle of his spade. "William Wilson?" he queried. There was a pause, as though he was letting the words roll round his mind.

I tried to help him by providing some additional information. "They also call him 'Herdwick Billy'." "Why didn't ta say so?" he remonstrated. And with a few hurried phrases he directed me to Herdwick View, near the outflow of Bassenthwaite Lake. Herdwick Billy, who settled here in 1932, met Beatrix at some of the Lakeland sheep shows. He also saw her at meetings of the Breeders' Association.

Herdwick Billy was, indeed, secretary when the first Flock Book was brought out in 1920. "There was some work in it, I can tell you." I was shown a copy of that first Flock Book, in which S D Stanley-Dodgson wrote: "A typical Herdwick sheep should primarily have a good strong coat of flowing wool, well carried out over the chest and hind legs, and the underside or belly well covered...The head should be carried high, broad across the forehead, deep in the jaw, wide at the nostrils, arched nose...The face should be grey or 'rimy' [hoar-frosted in appearance]; body round and deep; chest prominent and wide; legs covered with strong bristly hair..."

Hardiness has been one of the breed's outstanding qualities. "A Herdwick can thrive on the scantiest herbage of the most rugged mountains. I've known a Herdwick be covered by snow for twenty-one days – and recover. The only time I was pushed to fodder them was in 1917, when I was at Watendlath. It's a real high-lying place. We had a tremendous bad winter that year. The Swaledale is a softer breed. I'd put the Scotch Blackface next to the Herdwick for toughness."

Herdwick Billy told me that many of the judges at old-time sheep shows went a good deal by the eye. The eye of the sheep, that is. "They looked for eyes that were sharp and bright. The ears, too, should be sharp. If one hangs its ears down like a hound, it's not so good." He liked sheep with well-sprung ribs.

I asked him if the Herdwick had an extra rib. He replied: "I've heard that argument till I'm sick and tired of it. I don't know, but quite a few of the old generation chaps would almost have fought with you if you said it hadn't." At first, the extra rib was claimed for a flock at the top end of Duddon Valley. The flockmasters at Ulpha and Seathwaite in particular believed it to be true."

The majority of the wool clipped from Herdwicks was too strong and dark for the best quality of cloth-making. It was mainly used for carpets and rough cloth. Billy had heard that some was exported to America. Herdwick skins were cured with saltpetre and alum and converted into rugs and mats. Skins were also used for making brats, or aprons, used at sheep-dipping time.

From Herdwick Billy I heard of a Herdwick custom known as "clouting the twinters". Through sheep-breeding, Beatrix – respectfully known to the farmfolk as Mrs Heelis – would hear much talk about basic biology. Shearlings that were not to be put to the ram because they were too young to rear a lamb had twinter-clouts [small cloths] placed at their

Tilberthwaite, in a quiet valley near Coniston.

Opposite: Herdwick tups, daubed with 'show red' at Wasdale Head.

rear quarters. These cloths were taken off in spring to be washed and ironed for another breeding season. Billy told me the clouts were made from old clothing or coarse sacking. Eventually, it was easier to fence the shearlings into a special portion of land where they could not be "got at".

Troutbeck village.

7: Troutbeck Park

In 1921, Beatrix bought the 2,000-acre Troutbeck Farm, and its stock of 1,000 Herdwicks. They had previously been owned by the Troutbeck Park Green Slate Company who, purchasing it in 1883, let it to John Leak for £340 per annum. The farm buildings impressed by their size and antiquity, though traces exist in the valley and on the fells of a much older way of life. Troutbeck Beck was spanned by an ancient bridge.

When the area was a park in the old sporting sense, deer were hunted by the lords of Kendal, who could also rely on fresh venison in the depth of winter. The deeds of the farm include a copy of Charles II's grant of the property, confirming that made by Charles I to Huddleston Philipson. Then, and in following years, there arose a large farmstead and associated buildings. Behind it, on a tongue of land, the wintering sheep occasionally intermingled with red deer from the Martindale stock.

Herdwick sheep speckled Ill Bell, Froswick and adjacent lands and seasonally formed a bleating host in the few dale-bottom fields. The shepherds of Troutbeck Park, on their rounds of the fells, met up with men from Hartsop and Kentmere for a grand sorting of stock.

Ernest Wilson, who farmed Troutbeck Park for 29 years, was living in a modern house high on the hillside at Ambleside when I chatted with him about Beatrix and her love of Herdwick sheep. When he took over the tenancy, there was not a tractor in sight. The few machines, and also a plough, were drawn by horses of moderate size, having been crossed with stock of the fell-going variety.

Ernest saw Mrs Heelis – as he knew her respectfully - at the Lakeland shows. She had died three years before they moved to Troutbeck Park in April, 1947. At that time all around them were the cores of snowdrifts from a February blizzard, then the worst in living memory. Ernest had two men to help him. Between them, they had a dozen dogs at their command - "the old fell type of dog, a barker." Sheep dip was mixed in the old boilers near the kitchen of the farm. The boilers had also been

Walls without mortar above Langdale.

Top: A neat row of capstones on a Lakeland drystone wall.
Bottom: A drystone waller at work.

used for making the salve that, when wool was parted, was applied by finger to the skin of sheep in a pre-winter routine.

When, in 1955, I first met Tom Storey, another notable denizen of Troutbeck Park, he was caring for Beatrix's sheep at Sawrey. He too was invited to take up an appointment at Troutbeck Park. Mrs Heelis met him at precisely 6 p.m., on a November Saturday, in 1926. Tom was attending a dozen Shorthorn cows for Noble Gregg at Town End, Troutbeck, knowing as he milked that the farmer was about to relinquish his services, having taken a farm at Tebay. At the new place he would need a boy, not a man, to assist him. Said Tom: "Noble had a boy at Town End, so he kept the boy and let me go."

Noble Gregg was known as a speedy milker. It took just over five minutes to milk a cow. At five o'clock, the cattle had been cleaned out, provided with tubs, hand-milked, then *fothered* [fed] for the night." Tom's work was done. Enter: Mrs Heelis. She had been driven to Town End in a brand-new, bull-nosed Morris Cowley. At the wheel was Tommy Christie, who lived at Colthouse. Tommy was a forester on the estate who "doubled up" as chauffeur.

Tom Storey was to recall his employer as "a little woman, and bonnie-looking." What was she dressed like? "Not like a lady. She wore an old herringbone costume, the skirt extending down to the ankles, a floppy sort of hat – and clogs on her feet. She never wore anything else on her feet but clogs. They were black, with clasps to fasten them." How did she get to know about the availability of Tom? News had spread that he was leaving Town End. Wanting a man to look after her sheep, she had gone round the district, asking the old farmers about his "character".

What she heard was to his credit. After asking Tom his name, she said: "Well, I'm Mrs Heelis. I hear you're leaving Mr Gregg's farm." Tom said: "Yes." She said: "Will you come and work for me?" Tom said: "Yes, I don't mind – if the money's right." Beatrix asked him his age. He replied: "I'm thirty." "Oh," she said, "I'm sixty." Just like that.

She asked him how much he was getting as a wage. She was quite straight about it. Tom told her. "Well," she said, "if you work for me I'll double it." Tom said it was all right. When could he start work for her? He was free on Monday and had nowhere else to go. "That was how it happened," said Tom, who was married with two young sons. "I went to Troutbeck Park on the following Monday."

The meeting with Mrs Heelis had come at the right time. Tom was able to continue to work with sheep. He said: "I'd always wanted to be a sheepman." Before he could settle in at Troutbeck Park, Beatrix asked him to take over at Hill Top, Sawrey. "She wanted to show Herdwick sheep. Why she couldn't show them from Troutbeck Park, I don't know, because there were about 1,000 Herdwick ewes there."

She had no other sheep but Herdwicks and, according to Tom, called the other breeds mongrels. When Tom said he would prefer to go to Troutbeck Park, she offered to augment his wage if he would manage the Sawrey farm instead. Tom said: "All right. If wife's willing, then I'm willing to move to Sawrey. That's how we landed…"

In fact, Tom was at Troutbeck Park for twelve months. He revealed that when Mrs Heelis had bought this farm, she thought that Englishmen were no good among sheep, so a Scotsman had been the first of her employees. Tom explained: "Her brother farmed in Scotland, you see. She got to know all about the Scottish ways, which were different from those we followed down here. She wanted the Scottish routine at Troutbeck Farm, but folk laughed at her. And she learned her lesson."

When she visited the farm, "it wasn't often she could be persuaded to come into t'kitchen for a drink o' tea. She just had her sandwiches, which were wrapped in a piece of paper. She ate 'em outside." While walking on the soggy high ground known as the Tongue, she carried a stick, not a crook. (Tongue was from an Old Norse word meaning "a ridge between two valleys that join"). She visited the fell in any sort of weather, sometimes with one of the collie dogs – with Nip or Fly, which were Artful Dodgers on the hills. They impressed her by their intelligence and obedience. She walked alone but was never lonely. "There was the company of gentle sheep, and wild flowers, and singing waters."

When Tom returned from kenning [looking at] the sheep, he would find her sitting at Tongue End, wanting to know all about his trip. To Beatrix, the Tongue was a place of silences and whispering echoes - a mighty tableland between two streams that rose together, north of the Tongue, in a maze of bogs and pools. One day, crouching behind a boulder, she watched four fell ponies circling in measured canter, their movements explaining to her the source of a host of unshod footprints, "much too small for horses' footmarks, much too round for deer or sheep."

It was said that the only person who frightened Beatrix was her chauffeur. When he was ready to leave the farm for the return to Sawrey, he would mention it to her. Once, 'tis said, she did not turn up immediately, so he left her. She wasn't late again! Beatrix did not mind fox-hunting, but no one had to pursue hares.

"A relation of hers was huntsman for a pack of harriers at Burneside, but she would not let him hunt at Troutbeck Park." The area was swarming with rabbits. Hawkshead fields, beyond Esthwaite Water extending to 70 acres, Jack Hird cleared them of rabbits by snaring them. One year he bagged 900 and sold them – thruppence a couple – to customers in Windermere and district.

At Troutbeck, Tom began work in November, which was tupping [mating] time for the sheep. "I put rams on to a thousand breeding ewes and I lambed them the following spring." To be precise, he marked 992 lambs, putting a red pop on the hook [where the thigh bone sticks up] to identify them as belonging to Troutbeck Park.

He continued: "You marked as many as you thought fit, and you forgot two or three that were left to lamb because fox would go with them...Troutbeck Park hadn't had much good luck with lambing. It was a devil of a farm for sheep fluke. There was no cure for it in those days...Cure came from a veterinary firm at Newcastle in the form of a capsule. By jove, we used it that back-end [autumn] and it was a life-saver."

Anthony Benson, a shepherd, had first worked at Troutbeck Park as a lad fresh from school. (The farm was then owned by Mrs Leach). He

Anthony Benson,
Beatrix's shepherd at
Troutbeck Park.

had a variety of jobs, and was working as a shepherd for Isaac Fleming. A shepherding job at Troutbeck Park was mentioned by Willie Heelis, who was Isaac's solicitor. Anthony came face to face with Mrs Heelis. He inquired about the wage he would receive. (Isaac had paid him 25s a week). She offered 50s "straight off". She also arranged for a cottage to be built for the Bensons. "She kept us in coal. She fed five or six dogs. So that wage was as good as 60s."

Anthony was a shepherd at Troutbeck Park for 15 years. He told me with mock gravity that in those 15 years she had never paid him. A pause. "She usually paid t'wife, saying that money should go into the home." He recalled that Beatrix was fond of an old dog called Bob. "It was a lile bow-legged thing, though it'd been a good dog in its time. I used to think that Bob was useless. But you had to take it with you."

When, one day, Anthony and the dog reached an area on the fell crossed by a sheep trod, Bob "wouldn't gang any further. It went along that trod and was never seen again…We wasted many a day looking for it. Mrs Heelis came up every day to help." There was a special kennel at Troutbeck Park for dogs that had been pensioned off; she inspected the kennel on every visit to the farm.

She was "a lish body" who loved to visit the fields where sheep were kept. Or she'd set off on a hill track. She was excited by sheep-clipping time, with its noise and bustle. "We clipped between 2,000 and 3,000 sheep – all Herdwicks, though on a fell-spot like Troutbeck it wasn't always easy to keep the flock pure wi' stray tups coming in from other places."

It took seven hours just to gather the sheep, which went as far as High Street. "Then I've seen us sit down of a morning at seven o'clock and clip, then git up and have our dinners, and back and sit down again, and clip till six o'clock. It went on maybe for a fortnight or three weeks. There were always four of us clipping. We fed well."

When the Tysons moved into the house at Troutbeck Farm, there were lots of features associated with Beatrix. She had supervised the installation of the fireplace in the living room – a fireplace made of local stone with sandstone pillars. It had been made by Mr Storey, a local builder. His son Charles, a lad at the time, recalled that she stood over father and told him where each stone was to go! Pieces from the old black-lead fireplace, including the recken, were incorporated in the new fireplace that Beatrix had made.

The house was tenanted by mice. Beatrix fed them. "You could be baking in the kitchen and they would run out of their holes and appear round the table. We tried catching them with bowls, but it was hopeless. Fortunately we haven't got them now." Outdoors, wildlife tended to be confiding. During the winter, a dozen or so red deer grazed the low ground. "You could look out of the window at dusk and there were deer not so far away." Badgers romped in a field, seeming to sense that no one was going to bother them. "They carried on playing about when people were walking on the lane."

Anthony recalled that at lambing time, an old Scotsman called Joe Mosscrop, noted for his care of waifs and strays, was invited by Beatrix to stay at Troutbeck Park. With him came his dog Jess. When he wanted it to do anything for him, he always said please. There was no electricity at the farm. At night, an old paraffin lamp provided the illumination. Beatrix thought the world of Joe. He was a good sheep doctor. Handed a chilled lamb, he put two or three drops of gin from a bottle on to its tongue to warm it up.

Anthony was one of those indomitable men who, in October, drove young sheep long distances from fell farms such as Troutbeck Park to winter grazings on land overswept by mild sea breezes. "We used to take sheep, mainly shearlings, to Home Fell at Coniston and Tarn Hows. The hoggs [last year's lambs] went on to Birker Moor." It was a massive operation that began from Troutbeck Park at first light. About 600 sheep, in two trips, were transferred to their winter quarters.

Controlling them on route would be two men with two or three dogs. The route took in Lowwood and Waterhead, thence over Rathay Brigg, up to Skelwith Brigg and over the top of Oxen Gill to Coniston. With nobbut a few sheep at Sawrey, they were moved no farther than Birker Moor. In April, the Birker Moor sheep were walked to Tilberthwaite, where "we'd stop aw neet." Lile Tommy Stoddart welcomed them to Tilberthwaite and put the men up overnight.

He was also available to help next morning when the quarries extending to the top of Oxen Fell must be negotiated. It was not unusual for the drovers to come under the steady gaze of Beatrix. "If you were on t'road wi' t'sheep, Mrs Heelis passed you three or four times to see that all was going well. If there was a lame dog, she'd pick it up, take it home and fetch you another dog. Mind you, if *you* were lame, she wouldn't do owt. She simply watched the droving operation from her car."

At Troutbeck Park, Galloway cattle were reared for beef. "We had only one milk cow, for household use. If that cow ran dry, they took it down to Hill Top and fetched another. We'd always plenty o' milk." The Galloways were from stock bought at Newcastleton, on the Borders. Anthony had "nowt to do" with cattle. "They used to take calves from Troutbeck to Newcastleton by motor wagon. Mrs Heelis would go to t'bull sale." While recuperating after a serious illness in the late 1930s, she paid periodic visits to her beloved Troutbeck Park and watched the sheep being clipped. She also visited her fine beef cattle – a white bull and some 30 cows, with calves at foot.

On one of my visits to Troutbeck Park, I entered a room which had rarely been entered since Beatrix used it as a study. Mrs Tyson mentioned its appearance when they first arrived. "The furniture was green mouldy and we had to make our way through cobwebs to find anything. A cotton carpet and little woollen rugs on the floor were preserved by being placed under a carpet that was subsequently fitted. The fire tongs and poker remained beside a fireplace she would have known."

Everything was just stacked up. "There was a picture that, we were told, was the favourite of Willie Heelis. It was an animal study and rather dark." In the bottom of a cupboard set against a wall was a pile of her drawings. "Little animals, scribbles, notes she had written." On a decorative writing desk stood a writing box on which there was a mother-of-pearl inlay. A glass-fronted case held a stuffed pine marten.

Troutbeck Park remained true to its Herdwicks, though the eastern areas of Lakeland were being invaded by the Swaledale, a more profitable breed. This new type had been fixed by selective breeding of stock on and around Tan Hill. Beatrix's insistence that stocks of Herdwicks should remain on the farms donated to the National Trust meant there was no argument about the local breed. Some of her tenants at Troutbeck Park would have preferred to deal with Swaledale sheep.

One such observed: "When you come to look at Herdwicks on the real Herdwick fells in the west – Eskdale, Wasdale – you find those at Troutbeck Park are half as big again. It's that much better going for them…" The herdwick was said to be a "picky" feeder. "They'd starve if they couldn't get their own food naturally. Hay is not very practical because if you take it to sheep on the fells there's so much wind you've lost it before you get started. Feed blocks helped the situation. A herdwick would eat a little bit."

A time-honoured custom among the farmers of Lakeland was the shepherds' meet, a time when any strays that had been taken up in a given area were, by reference to horn burns and marks, claimed by their owners. Canon Rawnsley, friend of the Potters, wrote about the Mardale

Clipping sheep at Gatescarth.

Shepherds' Meet in a book published in 1906. I found myself comparing his account (which ended abruptly with the flooding of the valley by Manchester Waterworks) with my experiences of a meet at Troutbeck (in which Beatrix was to have a territorial interest with her purchase of the big sheep farm of Troutbeck Farm in 1921).

Consider Rawnsley's account of the Mardale gathering in Edwardian times. At least once a year, he wrote, in a reasonably good attempt at capturing the flavour of local dialect, but without the apostrophes, Mardale has "a gay good getherin o fwoke fra far and near." On the third Saturday in November, determined to combine pleasure with business, "a hunt is organised, and after the sheep are sorted out and claimed, the rest of the day is spent in merriment and cheer."

Rawnsley "learned that the shepherds' meeting at Mardale 'wasn't founded in't memory of man.'" Shepherds devoted a week to "raking" the fells and bringing down to the *Dun Bull* the sheep that were not their own. A guide existed giving the distinctive *lug* and *smit* marks of the various flocks. It was seldom referred to, for "all the shepherds ken the marks as well as they ken their own bairns...Poor little unclaimed Herdwick! What a picture of forlornness! Surely the scapegoat in the wilderness was not much more forlorn than the friendless sheep that none could own, sent back to the winter mountains."

In 1962, at the Troutbeck Shepherds' Meet, several species of sheep were involved. The practical object of the Meet being to bring together stray sheep, sort them and return them to their owners, that year rather more than 40 sheep stood, miserably, with matted fleeces, in a small croft near the hotel. A Rough Fell sheep that had been "taken up" was seen, by its markings, to belong to a farm in Kentmere, three miles away, o'er t'tops.

Meanwhile, grey sheets of rain swept up the Troutbeck valley with such weight and frequency I could not be certain just where earth met sky. Water gurgled down the steep fell slopes, frothing like milk in a cooler. It gushed from overworked guttering on the farms, inns and cottages. Khaki-tinted torrents poured from the lanes. The lowest part of the valley glinted steely-grey from floodwater.

Anthony Chapman had led his Coniston foxhounds on to the fells. A supporter who remained behind said: "I'm capped he lowsed today. It's going to be terrible. Hardly fit for sheep." John Bulman, of the Windermere Harriers, had a van containing 13 couple hounds. They were not to be released. John didn't want any scared sheep rushing into swollen becks.

During the day, the business of the strays was satisfactorily sorted out. There had been a hunt. A fox put up on Robin Crag was lost, the hounds were recovered and the hunters returned, damp but cheerful. There was a desirable snugness at the *Queen's Head Hotel.* On the menu was Hot Pot and Chilled Mutton. At the inn, most of the men already had the inner warmth of ale and spirits. I saw an ornate bar fashioned from an Elizabethan four-poster bed that once stood in Appleby Castle.

The hotel staff and farmers' wives attended to a savoury hot-pot that was at the last stage of preparation in the Mayor's Parlour upstairs. Into the hotpot went 40 lb of mutton, a hundredweight of potatoes, three stones each of carrots and onions, and about 30 black puddings. And into that upper room and its neighbours, on the evening of the Shepherds' Meet, crowded over 100 people, talking and drinking and singing until their throats were dry – then drinking again.

In an area where entertainment is rarely organised, this was an opportunity for social activity, a brief change from the stresses of farm, weather and stock. "Not many old cards are left now," said one shepherd, "but you'll meet those who remain at the annual Shepherds' Meet. You can hear a bit o' real Westmorland twang as well. Take a good look around, mister. In another fifty years – 'appen less – you'll doubtless see nowt like this."

The hotpot was ready. Some of us knew before we sat down it might be a day or two before our ribs settled back into place. There was a long table, set out with the usual cutlery and also with huge jars of pickles, piccalilli and beetroot. The hotpot was a real Westmorland blend of the various foodstuffs. It was succeeded by pie and custard, followed in turn by good strong tea. In the evening, the merriment began with laughter, tale-telling and song.

8: Her Last Days

For pleasure, and certainly not to order, Beatrix put down the pen for the last time at the age of sixty-eight. She had enjoyed taking pains over her writing, remarking that "my usual way of writing is to scribble and cut out, and write it again and again. The shorter and plainer the better...I polish! polish! polish! - to the last revise." She wrote to a friend in 1934: "I am written out for story books and my eyes are tired for painting."

Josephina told me of a never-to-be-forgotten day in 1937 when Beatrix visited Delmar and herself at their rented accommodation, which was Heathwaite Farm above Coniston. "Her funny old car was too rickety to go up the steep lane, so we met her at the bottom with a milk float and white pony. The step was too high for her so we laid a board across. Delmar held one hand. I held the other little podgy hand. She walked up this board into the float and took the reins and then the milkman's boy held the bridle.

"There was this wonderful procession up the lonnin [lane] and all the people in the cottages on the way knew about it. She held the reins and went up, quite a long way, and they all waved through the windows. And when we got to Heathwaite Farm, we found the local people had sent bunches of flowers. The farm was full of flowers. Oh – they loved her all right." The Banners provided lunch. Beatrix had second helpings of everything.

In the following year, Delmar painted his celebrated portrait of Beatrix, complete with cherubic smile. The painting was not done from life; she lacked the patience to sit still for long. She is portrayed wearing Herdwick cloth. She clutches an umbrella – the one that belonged to Norman Warne. Visitors to Hill Top see the original painting. A copy reposes in the National Portrait Gallery in London.

**Delmar Banner's celebrated portrait of Beatrix on a
Lakeland showfield. (© National Portrait Gallery, London)**

Beatrix in old age with Alison Hart. The Peke was the last dog owned by Beatrix.

Her life in Lakeland had been neatly divided into two parts - a shy spinster, writer and artist, who made birds and animals lovable to children by dressing them up in clothes to engage in novel antics, and the redoubtable Mrs Heelis, farmer and conservationist, keen to ensure by her purchases that Lakeland would keep its green and pleasant landscape.

When Girl Guides visited her property from the late 1920s, she had a minor grumble when girls were inclined to drop hair "slides", buttons and paper in the hay. A dairymaid picked over the hay before it could reach the mouths of the livestock – and was allowed to keep the booty. Beatrix was community-minded. She founded the Hawkshead Nursing Association which introduced a District Nurse to the area, providing her with a cottage and sustaining her partly through funds raised at a sale of work.

Letters from Beatrix to Josephina Banner which I was able to read included one dated October 20, 1938, when Beatrix returned a book about rural crafts and expressed sadness "that the old strong honestly-made hand crafts are dwindling... The smithy in this village is closed, and not for want of work. There are still a few good wheelwrights left: but I observe with disgust the increasing use of rubber motor tyres on carts and wheelbarrows. They offer some advantages, but no one can call them lovely on a farm horse-drawn cart..."

Beatrix was finding it curious how graphic children could be up to a certain age. "Then they lose it, or it is wiped out by teaching. A shepherd's child about five years ago showed me a remarkable crayon scribble of two lambs...remarkably capering lambs kicking up their heels. I asked for another specimen. Now, six months later, she gave me a 'picture' done at school: outline traced from an elaborate scene in Kate Greenaway style, little boy and girl, cottages, etc., all carefully coloured, and consigned to the fire by me..."

The outbreak of the 1939-45 war brought an immediate response from Willie. He would be a reserve policeman, while refusing to don a "tin hat". He brought his special knowledge of rural affairs to the War Agricultural Committee. In a letter written on November 9, 1939,

Beatrix commented on what had been "a most lovely autumn for those who had leisure to enjoy the beautiful of the peaceful valleys and fells. For my part, between arrears consequent on being laid up, and wanting to do as much as might before petrol is scarce, I have hardly known which way to turn during October."

Visiting Little Langdale, she had discussed repairs at various farms. There was not much ploughing to be done on sheep farms but timber and pit props were a pressing need. "A lot will have to be cut; it wants careful choosing…It's not a cheerful time. A most peculiar war; for those of us who lived through the last one, it seems different; 'bad to reckon up' as the saying is. And everything in a muddle. There is no use thinking; keep working and make the best of things!"

Food and petrol were rationed. Peter Rabbit's descendants were stalked by a hungry populace. German prisoners were held in a camp at Grizedale Hall, just over the hill from Sawrey.   A tractor appeared and with ancillary equipment traversed a hayfield. It was not to Beatrix's satisfaction. She was seen scuffling about near the hedges that bordered the field, pulling bits of hay into the open. Wool prices improved. The Ministry of Agriculture insisted on her growing potatoes at Troutbeck Park.

Enemy aircraft on bombing missions to the shipyards of Barrow droned across the night sky and on the return journey off-loaded the remaining bombs, most of which fell on open ground or water. A terrible exception was the destruction of a remote farmhouse, with much loss of life. The crew of one plane that crashed in the depths of winter died on impact. Frozen, their bodies were found dangling in their harnesses from the crags. Just north of Bowness was a factory where Sunderland Flying Boats were assembled, to be flown off the lake.

Josephina told me of her last meeting with Beatrix. They walked beside the flower garden, then beside the apple trees and the vegetables, reaching a strip of ground festooned with wild flowers that Beatrix had collected and replanted. "Among them was zig-zag clover, of which she picked a leaf to show me." The two ladies approached the same little iron gate, set between mossy posts, where clover had been featured in the tale.

Josephina recalled: "She pulled my head down to her level and she kissed me. Neither of us spoke. We knew, as we parted company, that we would never meet again. When I turned round, there was Beatrix, waving a clover leaf at me – just like Timmy Willie had done."

Beatrix was not to see the war's ending. Near Christmas, 1943, as her life ebbed away, the weather was cold and miserable. Tom Storey was summoned to her bedside. "Mrs Rogerson told me she wanted to see me. Would I come across after I'd finished the farm work? I said: 'Aye, I'll be across'. I finished hand-milking at about six o' clock. Then I went into t'house and had a wesh and a bite to eat – what we called supper. I didn't change all through, but just put a decent jacket on. Mrs Rogerson saw me into t'house."

Willie Heelis was not at home. "Beatrix lay in bed. I sat down. We chatted about farming. She asked how things were going on. I think she thought she was 'going' the way she talked to me that night. One thing she asked me to do – and I thought it was the main thing she had asked me to come across for – was to carry on looking after the farm for Mr Heelis after her day. Two years before she died, when she was ill in hospital, I'd had a letter asking me to do the same thing."

Tom left her bedside at about seven o'clock. Beatrix Heelis (nee Potter) died during the night, December 22, 1943, aged 77. She was cremated at Blackpool on the last day of the year. In due course, one lunchtime, Willie Heelis arrived at Hill Top with her ashes, wrapped in newspaper. He handed them over to Tom, who had just sat down to his Christmas dinner. Said Willie: "You'll know where these have to go, Storey."

Tom finished his meal, had the usual sit-down, then went for a walk with the parcel that Willie Heelis had brought. "It was a bonny day. I scattered the ashes on one of the Hill Top high pastures. I was told not to say just where. Otherwise, visitors would be all over the place." About 18 months later, Tom was scattering the ashes of Willie Heelis. He had been devastated by his wife's death. He left most things in Castle Cottage as they had been when Beatrix was alive.

Just where were the ashes of Beatrix spread? Possibly on an intake above her beloved Hill Top. I got a hint from Josephina when she was living – alone in her extreme old age – in a small flat behind Prince Charlie's House, Stricklandgate, Kendal. In February, 1988, I received a letter from her. She complimented me on a book I had written using first-hand accounts from some of those who knew her. It was, wrote Josephina, the best Beatrix Potter book – along with that written by Margaret Lane.

Josephina's letter included these lines: "Do come here when you can (they will show you up to my studio). There are things I'd like to talk around...An incident at Low Park. And WHY did she choose that Satter Howe meadow as a memorial? I can't walk much now and very badly want to know what view and surroundings it has. Very apt <u>Saeter</u> (Norse to the bone)." In her will, Beatrix desired that a meadow at Satter Howe, on Ferry Hill, should be kept in memory of local men who died in the Great War. Margaret Lane, in *The Magic Years of Beatrix Potter*, included in a caption to one of Beatrix's paintings of Jemima Puddleduck "the field at the edge of Jemima's wood where Beatrix Potter's ashes were eventually scattered."

A death notice in *The Westmorland Gazette* mentioned: "Cremation private. No mourning, no flowers and no letters, please."

Beatrix bequeathed almost all her possessions to her husband during his lifetime. Sums of money were left to two cousins. Her shares in the publishing firm of Frederick Warne were left to Frederick Warne Stephens. On the death of Willie Heelis, he would also acquire the rights and royalties relating to her books. Remembered in her will were personal friends and helpers, including Tom Storey and her chauffeur Walter Stephens.

Tom enjoyed his years working for a celebrated landowner. "She was a good person to work for. She could be funny. You could meet her, and she'd never look sideways. Another time she would stop and talk to you. But she never had a long conversation with you." My last visit to Tom turned out to be – the last. Arriving at his cottage home, I rapped my knuckles against the door and listened for his ever-bright "Come in". This time the response was delayed.

I glanced through the window. Tom's favourite chair was empty. I heard a faint call, inviting me to enter. Tom lay in bed, suffering from an old chest complaint. A few weeks before, he had told me of his impending ninetieth birthday. It was, indeed, his birthday. We celebrated, Tom and I, with glasses of sherry. We chatted for a while until members of his family arrived with gifts and good wishes. On my next visit to Sawrey, I heard, alas, that Tom was dead and buried. He had died aged 90.

As for Willie Heelis, his death was prolonged and painful. He had accommodation at Purey Cust Chambers, almost in the shadow of York Minster and well within hearing of the dolorous notes of the largest bell as it proclaimed noontide. I regularly attended best-kept village committee meetings here but for Willie it was a nursing home. Suffering from prostrate gland trouble, he had a sad physical decline.

Tom Storey saw him just before he died in 1945. When Tom returned to the family home at Sawrey, he said: "I could tell he was a long way on…"

Janet Rawlins

9: Beatrix Remembered

Beatrix will not be forgotten as long as her little books circulate the world over. Anyone who reads them discovers there is magic in ordinary things - in rabbits and ducks, rhubarb patches and water-butts, white-washed cottages and lily-covered tarns, roadside flowers, pigs and goats and, of course, in Herdwick sheep.

Susan Ludbrook, the first custodian at Hill Top, meeting Beatrix for the first and last time in 1939, was left with an impression of a person of great delicacy and kindness. As custodian she was assisted by Freda Jackson, daughter of Tom Storey. In 1966, Susan Ludbrook recalled for readers of *Cumbria* her association with Hill Top, which had been opened informally in 1946. A few people interested in the National Trust gathered by personal invitation.

The house was subsequently open to villagers, friends and to any who had known Beatrix and wished to pay tribute to her memory. It was then decided to open the house for a prescribed period. A trickle of visitors found enchantment in features known to Beatrix – the wicket-gate, flagged path, old stone porch and oak door. In the kitchen they saw a wide chimney and old dresser. An imposing staircase led to a landing and an oak-framed bed on which naughty kittens had played. Best of all was a room with two fair-haired dolls and a doll's house, with everything just as it had been arranged by Beatrix herself.

Beatrix Potter with Herdwick sheep (painting by Janet Rawlins).

Ten thousand visitors, one in six being children, attended in the summer of 1946. From Easter next year, it was open to view for a full season. That spring saw the publication of Margaret Lane's book, *The Tale of Beatrix Potter*, which was written with the consent of Willie Heelis. The book, also published in America, became a best-seller.

Susan Ludbrook took special pleasure in making the old brasswork gleam. Freda, who loved the garden and knew Beatrix's taste in flowers, kept the rooms florally colourful. Margaret Lane visited Hill Top. So did Graham Sutton, the Lakeland novelist. H V Morton spent a day in the house with a photographer, preparing an article for the *National Geographical Magazine*. The "aunties" from BBC Children's Hour brought a group of children and broadcast from Hill Top. Wilfred Pickles invited Freda to join him in a radio programme.

In May, 1951, Leslie Linder – that shy and modest man - paid his first visit, which was spread over three days. Susan recalled: "I soon discovered that under his quiet manner and unassuming approach was a specialised interest in the Beatrix Potter stories and in her art as applied to children's education."

Leslie wished to compile and publish a book to be entitled *The Art of Beatrix Potter*. This would be annotated and made available to students and other interested folk. "It was not to be a second biography as this side had been admirably covered by Margaret Lane...It was to be a companion book, showing Beatrix Potter as an artist in many more fields than her stories and throwing light on what had become known as The Hidden Years."

Not until the following season, 1952, did Leslie Linder return to Hill Top, staying with Mrs Kenyon in the corner house across from the Tower Bank Arms – the building which had been the village shop when Beatrix wrote her story of *Ginger and Pickles*. A limited edition of 5,000 copies of *The Art of Beatrix Potter* was published at four guineas. It was quickly sold out. Leslie Linder visited Hill Top again in 1957, presenting another copy of the book to Hill Top. He was induced to sign it.

Leslie spent part of his holiday in 1959 at Hill Top; he and his sister,

Enid, worked on cataloguing the manuscripts, being intrigued by a parcel that had not previously been examined. It was a bundle of old exercise books with odd leaves interspersed. One on the top appeared to be in German. The whole bundle was tied with string. When the book top had been removed, the rest appeared to be in code.

He submitted the code to experts but the few clues from the Beatrix fragments fitted into no known or accepted sequence. Leslie began to despair of ever unlocking the secret. On an Easter evening, he had a last try, found a clue and began the patient de-coding, magnifying, arranging and assembling the material into a consecutive narrative. The work was spread over four years. The hidden years of Beatrix Potter/Heelis were revealed in the *Journal*, which was published in 1966 - centenary year.

Sir Frederick Ashton, fascinated by her stories, choreographed and danced in a film entitled *Tales of Beatrix Potter* with the support of the Royal Ballet. A recent film, with a DVD as a follow up, was simply entitled *Miss Potter*, tracing her life from childhood in London and her ultimate settlement in Lakeland. In this biopic, Beatrix was played, sensitively, by Renée Zellweger, an American actress. For her, arriving in the Lake District "brought the whole Miss Potter story to life."

In my research about the real Beatrix Potter, I depended greatly on the assessment and memories of a dozen people, among them the astonishing Josephina Banner, who was still sculpting at the age of ninety-one. In my quest for Beatrix Potter, I had met fascinating people in thoroughly Lakeland settings. When Delmar Banner died, his widow, Josephina, had a variety of lodgings, including a cottage on the high side of Ambleside.

Having an appointment to join her for afternoon tea, at dusk, on a calm, dry November day I glanced through the curtainless window and saw Josephina sitting at the fireside in a living room furnished with antiques, including an old circular table with three places set for afternoon tea. Who was the mystery guest? She greeted me warmly. We were joined by Heaton Cooper, the artist. The main topic of discussion was, of course, Beatrix Potter. After the Ambleside cottage days, she had found a studio-cum-living quarters in a large building just inside the high wall of a local estate. Visiting her with Nigel Holmes of *Radio Cumbria*, I was told that large blocks of stone delivered to her studio were lifted over an intervening high wall by mobile crane!

I asked how the sculptress had found, in old age, the strength to do major work? She replied: "I am quite young inside and old outside. I find that being old is rather like feeling as you do after an operation in hospital. You wonder why you're so weak...It isn't so much a matter of strength; it's one of rhythm. I've done work for many years...It's not a strain; it's just a pleasant exercise."

In 1934, Beatrix gave a host of watercolours and drawings of fungi, mosses and fossils to the Armitt Library in Ambleside. On her death in 1943, the National Trust received a goodly number of mainly dalehead farms, with around 25,000 Herdwick sheep. A major acquisition was the Monk Coniston Estate, which Beatrix had bought in 1930. With a total acreage of 4,000, it extended from Coniston to Little Langdale. Within it was Tarn Hows, a tract of landscape, with a mountain backdrop. It is regarded as Lakeland scenery at its best, though the lake was dammed for industry in the valley and the setting is composed of upstart conifers.

Beatrix left Hill Top and its contents to the National Trust with the proviso that it be kept exactly as it was, complete with her furniture and china. It should also be open to the public. The National Trust also came into the possession of the nearby *Tower Bank Arms*. Margaret Lane, who wrote the first major biography of Beatrix, also prepared the National Trust's little booklet for Hill Top.

In it she wrote: "As a farmer, Beatrix Potter began buying pieces of land, cottages, 'intakes', little farms, and each part of the surrounding hills as she went to and fro on her business to fairs and sales. And, as a landowner who loved the Lakes, and saw only too clearly how hideously they were threatened by the exploiter and the jerry-builder, she became convinced that the only sure defence lay in ownership by the National Trust. So she began buying farm property with increasing care and imagination, always with one eye on the National Trust, for which she ultimately intended it."

I last spoke with Josephina in her little flat behind an antique shop in Stricklandgate, Kendal. She was 93 years of age. We talked our way back down the years to a time known to Beatrix. Said Josephina: "The old way of life has gone; Lakeland humour remains…like a good old crust of brown bread. With a bit of spice added." I mentioned *The Bield*. How did they acquire it? "These things are not sold on the market. They are sold just talking over a gate."

Until after her death, Beatrix was never known locally as Beatrix Potter. That was her maiden name and therefore not to be used when respectful people addressed her. It was as Mrs Heelis that she spent virtually all her Lakeland years. She was a superb naturalist. Long after her death, the respected and influential Linnean Society issued a posthumous public apology for discriminating against her a century before. The society had rejected biological research papers by her simply because she was a woman.

Her knowledge of how furred and feathered creatures lived and worked was clearly based on the death and dissection of the subjects. Such activity among the scientifically inclined did not raise any eyebrows in Victorian days. Her knowledge of wildlife was more extensive than this suggests. In her *Journal* entries for Sawrey, she recorded watching a hedgehog and playing with Peter Rabbit.

My quest for Beatrix revealed many facets about her life among us. Not all of them were praiseworthy. No one is perfect. Go to Sawrey at any time, and you will not walk alone. An interest in Beatrix's work in the place where she spent the last 30 years of her life rises to Pottermania on sunny days. When I closed my notebook and switched off my tape recorder for the last time, I turned pleasurably to a poem written by Lydia Thomas, one of my favourite contributors to *Cumbria* magazine:

Your eyes were always summer,
Common sense, surprise and fun
burnished your internal sun,
lighting your books. Here we find
a cradling-comfort, cats purr
warmth, recognising objects
homely, simple as bee skeps,
tea-pots, feathers, water-butts,
nests with eggs, a fox who struts
sneering across our dreaming,
first lesson about deceiving.

Clogs on feet, dressed in tweed
conversing with farmers, owt
about sheep, but Herdwicks' breed
you judged. There can be nowt
worth knowing, you didn't know,
which is why my children's
children stand at my bookshelf
and find their hands go
to Beatrix Potter.

The 'Little Books' of Beatrix Potter (1900-30)

Beatrix was described by Judy Taylor, an authority on her life and work, as "an intriguingly fascinating woman." Having a mainly solitary childhood, in a big house in London, Beatrix had fallen back on her own resources, becoming inventive and creative. Her first effort, concerning Peter Rabbit, was compiled when she was in her thirties; the book was succeeded over eleven years by eighteen others, two of the stories being produced in panoramic, pull-out form.

Initially, Beatrix underplayed her commercial success, observing: "I am aware that these little books don't last long, even if they are a success." She based books on pet animals, some being smuggled into the house and others observed when the family was holidaymaking in Scotland or the Lake District. Wooden boxes were made to accommodate mice and rabbits. By bestowing human characteristics on pet animals and birds – rats, ducks among them - and devising unforgettable storylines, Beatrix held the attention of children the world over. A commercial spin-off from the original stories were such novelties as plates, mugs and pop-up books.

She became fond of the Lakeland type of farming, preferring grassy hills rather than the big, stern fells that formed a backdrop in almost every Lakeland scene. Having bought Hill Top, at Sawrey, her book about Tom Kitten and Samuel Whiskers was linked with that place. Mrs Tiggy-Winkle, hedgehog-washerwoman, enacted her life in the Newlands Valley, with Catbells as a backdrop. The tale featuring Jemima Puddle-Duck was enacted with Tower Bank Arms, at Sawrey, in mind. The Owl Island of the tale relating to Squirrel Nutkin was based on St Herbert's Island, Derwentwater.

These were not intended to be "cuddly" stories. In the tale about Mr Tod, the fox, there's trouble between him and Tommy Brock, the badger. The last-named steals the Flopsy Bunnies, grandchildren of Mr Bouncer Bunny, with the object of cooking and eating them. (They escape!). Her writing tailed off around 1920, one reason being a declining eyesight.

Derwentwater, showing one of the launches used for pleasure cruises.

Opposite: A shop window at Hawkshead.

Beatrix's stories, initially printed in black and white, but mostly with illustrations glowing with colour, were translated from standard English into languages as diverse as Latin, Welsh and Japanese. Their long-term popularity is assured.

1901-2 *The Tale of Peter Rabbit.* The title originally included *and Mr McGregor's Garden.* Peter, one of two favourite rabbits, was acquired when the Potters were holidaymaking at Dunkeld, in Scotland. The real Peter died, in his ninth year, in January, 1901. The *Tale*, first of many, had its genesis as the subject of a story-letter written for the ailing Noel Moore, a son of Annie Carter, her governess. Having puzzled about what she should write to the sick lad, Beatrix outlined a story concerning four little rabbits: Flopsy, Mopsy, Cottontail and Peter.

When a book version was proposed, Noel kindly loaned Beatrix the picture-letter she had sent him. With little interest shown by several publishers who had been approached, it was printed privately in 1901. Frederick Warne acquired Beatrix's "bunny book" in the following year. They made a success of it in the small picture-book market. Beatrix re-worked the monotone illustrations in colour. The Warne edition, planned to be marketed in October, 1902, sold out before publication.

1902-1903 *The Tailor of Gloucester.* Beatrix's favourite "little book" is a costumed romance, set in Gloucestershire, a break with her beloved Lakeland. Beatrix intended this work as a Christmas present for Freda Moore, daughter of her governess. Beatrix knew the city of Gloucester well, having stayed with relatives living at Harescombe Grange, near Stroud. Sketches in an exercise book led to the development of a fantasy based on a true local story – of a tailor named John Samuel Pritchard who was hired to make a waistcoat for the Mayor. Beatrix added mice to her version of the story, which was printed privately in 1902 – a time when Messrs Warnes were about to publish *Peter Rabbit*. A Warne edition of *The Tailor* was issued in 1903.

1903 *The Tale of Squirrel Nutkin.* A somewhat violent tale, it evolved from yet another a picture-letter, this being posted to Norah Moore, daughter of a former governess, in 1901. It was a time when the Potters had leased Lingholm, on the shores of Derwentwater, for their lengthy summer stay. Lingholm estate was in prime red squirrel terrain. To work on the book, Beatrix borrowed the letter back and produced a revised version in which Nutkin, an impertinent squirrel, had joined his brother Twinkleberry and many cousins, sailing to Owl Island [in real life, St Herbert's Island] to collect nuts from the hazel trees. The makeshift boats were tiny rafts made of twigs. They placaded Old Brown (an owl), the main resident, with gifts of food, including dead mice and minnows. The perverse Nutkin annoyed Old Brown by singing a daft riddle. The owl retaliated by capturing Nutkin with the object of skinning him alive. Nutkin escaped, minus most of his tail. Beatrix arranged for the commuting squirrels to use their tails as sails. This was probably an adaptation of an idea from America, where squirrels were said to use this technique when crossing rivers.

1904 *The Tale of Benjamin Bunny.* Benjamin was Beatrix's first pet rabbit. The story, an unadorned tale, of special appeal to youngsters, was dedicated to "the children of Sawrey from old Mr Bunny."

1904 *The Tale of Two Bad Mice.* An amusing tale, this is basically a girls' book. It features a doll's house, photographs of which – together with dolls and furnishings – were provided by Norman Warne, to whom Beatrix would become engaged but who, alas, died in August of the following year, aged 37. The storyline deals with the exploits of Tom Thumb and Hunca Munca, two mice who break into a dolls' house in the temporary absence of its occupants. The house is trashed.

Order is restored when the small girl who owns the house buys a policeman doll and her nurse invests in a mousetrap. Tom Thumb pays to replace the objects he damaged. Hunca Munca cleans the dolls' house every morning. Beatrix had a good friend, Winifred Warne, in mind when she penned this tale.

1905 *The Tale of Mrs Tiggy-Winkle.* A hedgehog pet, having numerous spikes, could not be classifiable as cuddly, yet Beatrix kept a pet hedgehog for years, being thus provided with references for the art work in this book. Mrs T-W was transformed as a washerwoman. The book was published at a sad time. Norman Warne, to whom Beatrix had

The island in Derwentwater visited by Squirrel Nutkin.

been engaged for less than a month, died from leukaemia. Mrs T-W's tale was dedicated to Luce, a vicar's daughter from Little-town, in the Newlands Valley, where the story was set. (Luce finds her lost hankie and "pinnie" in Mrs Tiggy-Winkle's laundry). Incidentally, the hedgehog which was the inspiration for Mrs Tiggy-Winkle became old and decrepit, being "put to sleep" and buried in the back garden of the Potters' home in London.

1905 *The Pie and the Patty-pan.* The intention of this book, which was dedicated to Joan, the sixth child of Annie Moore, was that it should be "read to Baby." Printed large size, the book was set in the village of Sawrey, where a pussy-cat named Ribby invited to tea a little dog called Duchess. (The book was reprinted by Warne in 1964 as *The Tale of the Pie and The Patty-Pan*).

1906 *The Tale of Mr Jeremy Fisher.* Norman Warne having died, his brother Harold took over the Beatrix Potter book work. Jeremy Fisher, originally a Scottish frog, began life – as did other Beatrix Potter creations - in a picture letter, written at Dunkeld in 1893. It was intended for Eric Moore. Beatrix changed the setting to Sawrey and based her story on several pet frogs she had closely studied. Jeremy became a dandy of the Regency period, in one scene being portrayed wearing a smart brown coat and reading a newspaper. He used a water-lily leaf as a boat. Beatrix's considerable knowledge of the natural world is evident in her fine background studies of water plants. Jeremy, portrayed with anatomical correctness, had a chancy life, including a close and potentially disastrous escape from the jaws of a large trout.

1906 *The Story of a Fierce Bad Rabbit* and *The Story of Miss Moppet* (panoramic, intended mainly for young children). They would later appear as books. The "bad rabbit" aspect was desired by Louie, the daughter of Harold Warne, to whom Peter Rabbit was too well behaved. She wanted to read about a naughty rabbit! The Miss Moppet story is of attempts by a cat to catch a mouse. She arouses the curiosity of the mouse by wrapping her head in a duster and sitting quietly before the fire. She watches him approach through a hole in the duster, captures him – but eventually loses him. The mouse made his escape through the hole in the duster!

1907 *The Tale of Tom Kitten.* Three little kittens, indeed. There is Tom, of course, and also Mittens and Moppet. As company is expected at the house, their mum, Tabitha Twitchit, tidies them up so they will be presentable. In the great outdoors they become dirty and lose their clothes to some puddle-ducks. So, back home, they are kept out of sight of the company, being hidden upstairs. The visitors are told they have measles. The story, set at Hill Top, Sawrey, has especially colourful illustrations, featuring garden plants in full bloom. Sawrey village is also portrayed. (Tabitha Twitchit was the name of a local cat).

1908 *The Tale of Jemima Puddle-Duck.* Jemima, a naïve duck, wearing a poke-bonnet and shawl, was created in a farmyard tale for Ralph and Betsy, children of John Cannon, who was Beatrix's manager at Hill Top Farm. Jemima, not allowed to keep eggs laid at the farm, seeks a safe place in the forest. She is coaxed into nesting in the home of a gentleman fox, who sends Jemima out and about to collect herbs used for duck-stuffing. The fox claims he needs the herbs for an omelette. Jemima is eventually rescued by Kep, a collie at Hill Top. (Incidentally, Mrs Cannon invariably raised her broods of ducklings under a hen!).

1908 *The Roly-Poly Pudding* (reprinted in 1926 as *The Tale of Samuel Whiskers or The Roly-Poly Pudding*). This book was dedicated to a long-dead (white) pet rat. When Beatrix bought Hill Top, it was rat-riddled. Cats were imported to deal with the problem. The story concerns Beatrix's aforementioned pet rat – and also features Farmer Potatoes, a real-life resident of Sawrey.

1909 *The Tale of the Flopsy Bunnies. (*A sequel to *Peter Rabbit* and *Benjamin Bunny*). Flopsy and Benjamin Bunny have numerous offspring and finding sufficient food is not easy. There are no spare cabbages at the home of Peter Rabbit, so a sortie is made to the rubbish heap of Mr McGregor – a heap with lots of overgrown lettuces. Having consumed as many as they could manage, the bunnies fell asleep. While still asleep, Mr McGregor slipped them into a bag, from which they escape through a hole nibbled by Thomasina Tittlemouse. Benjamin and Flopsy refill the bag with vegetables that are rotten. Mr McGregor, taking this load home, is scolded by his wife.

1909 *Ginger and Pickles.* First written as a Christmas present for Louie Warne, the title was subsequently changed to *The Tale of Ginger and Pickles*, the venue being a Sawrey shop belonging to John Taylor. In Beatrix's tale, the shop is run by a tom cat and a terrier and the book takes in some characters from the author's previous "little books".

1910 *The Tale of Mrs Tittlemouse.* A New Year gift for Nellie Warne, daughter of Harold Warne. The main character is a woodmouse living in a bank under a hedge. Home-proud, she incessantly swept the sandy floors and, as an early example of her pride, was upset when a beetle that had lost its way left marks from its dirty feet. A spider was rebuked for leaving ends of cobwebs. Also in the book is Mr Jackson, whose home was in a drain in a wet ditch. He was discouraged because he never wiped his feet. The cleaning fever lasted the book through. Dealing with a bee's nest was a problem. When a party was held for five other little mice, Mr Jackson, who had helpfully removed the bee's nest, was not invited.

1911 *The Tale of Timmy Tiptoes.* With characters including chipmunks and a bear (!), this book had a special appeal for young American readers.

1912 *The Tale of Mr Tod.* Tod is an old name for fox. The fox of the title is nomadic, bad-tempered, inhabiting the hills around Sawrey. In fact, the story concerns two disagreeable animals – the aforementioned Mr Tod and Tommy Brock (badger). Mr Tod commutes between several homes. Tommy Brock becomes an unwelcome squatter. He also steals the grandchildren of Mr Bouncer Bunny, intending to make a meal of them. They are tracked down by Benjamin Bunny, their dad, and their cousin. To cut short a longer-than-usual tale, which is illustrated with fewer than usual colour pictures – the grandchildren escape! – Beatrix dedicated the book to the infant son of Caroline Hutton, a cousin who was married to the Laird of Ulva, which is a small Hebridean island.

1913 *The Tale of Pigling Bland.* This appeared shortly before Beatrix married Willie Heelis and became increasingly fond of Lakeland farming and she noticed some pigs had joined the animal population of Hill Top. (A tiny black girl-pig that was not wanted by farm manager John

Cannon had slept in a basket by Beatrix's bed and was bottle-fed as it grew to independence!). Pigling Bland – and Alexander, his brother – suffered from a food shortage. There was not enough to feed the piglets. The plot evolves with Alexander getting into trouble with the police and Pigling Bland, seeking the brother, being lost in the woods. At a farm, the pig is benighted in an unfamiliar chicken coop. He is found by the farmer, befriended by the black pig and, adventurously, escapes to freedom.

1918 *The Tale of Johnny Town-Mouse.* Based on an Aesop fable, this story is given a Lakeland flavour by being set near Hill Top, Sawrey. The tale concerns Timmy Willie, a rural mouse, born in a garden. Peckishness and curiosity led him to creep through a hole in the large hamper used by the gardener for despatching vegetables to town via a carrier. Timmy, falling asleep, awakes in town! Johnny Town-Mouse (long tail) introduces Timmy Willie (shortish tail) to some of his friends when the visiting mouse gatecrashes their dinner party. Johnny eventually persuades Timmy to return to his natal area in the hamper which, regularly, is "returned to sender".

1929 *The Fairy Caravan.* This was to be the longest, also the most personal book, printed privately, then – having been passed over by Warnes – published in Philadelphia by David McKay. Local scenes include Troutbeck Park, Beatrix's most extensive sheep farm. (The book was first published in England in 1952).

1930 *The Tale of Little Pig Robinson.* A book published on both sides of the Atlantic, the American edition containing the greatest number of illustrations.

Lakeland Haunts of Beatrix Potter

Ambleside. The Armitt Library, in Rydal Road, has an important collection of watercolours donated by Beatrix in 1943. Here are over 450 watercolours – fungi, microscopic, natural history, archaeology. The Library is open every day (Christmas excepted) from 10 a.m to 5 p.m.

Colthouse. Beatrix occasionally joined the Quakers at the old Meeting House built in 1688 at Colthouse, near Hawkshead. Simple and unadorned, Quaker-style, it stands in its own walled grounds. Nearby is a separate Quaker burial ground where, on sloping ground, the gravestones are seen to be of the Quaker form – simple slab, rounded top.

Crosthwaite Church. The present church, dedicated to St Kentigern (who was also known as St Mungo) dates from 1523 but its foundation is much earlier. In 1883, after a spell at Wray, H D Rawnsley became Vicar. During his Crosthwaite years, he – with Miss Octavia Hill and Sir Robert Hunter – founded the National Trust, its object being to purchase and preserve, for the nation, places of natural beauty and historic interest. Inscribed on a wall memorial at Crosthwaite to Rawnsley are the words "who battled for the true and just."

Eskdale. Beatrix's fascination with Lakeland agricultural shows began with a visit to Eskdale, a lakeless valley in western Lakeland. The River Esk terminates in an estuary at Ravenglass. In 1935, Beatrix bought Penny Hill Farm.

Esthwaite Water. The Potter family had a holiday stay at Lakefield (now known as Ees Wyke), overlooking Esthwaite Water, the most changed of all the major lakes. Esthwaite Water, which has been designated a site of special scientific interest, covers an area of 280 acres, having deep basins and shallow bays. In summer, there is a profusion of water lilies. Nutrient-rich, it is a notable trout fishery, being also celebrated for its pike, the record fish caught making the scales dip at rather more than 39 lb.

Friends Meeting House at Colthouse. A Unitarian, Beatrix occasionally worshipped with the Quakers.

Waterhead, Ambleside.

Fawe Park, Derwentwater, where the Potters had their annual holiday in 1903. It was here that Beatrix developed an idea for compiling a book about Benjamin Bunny, who in literary terms was Peter Rabbit's cousin!

Hawkshead. Examples of her work might be seen in the Beatrix Potter Gallery, in Main Street. The gallery was opened in 1988, the premises having been used for many years by William Heelis, the solicitor.

Hill Top, her first Lakeland home, purchased in 1905. She used royalties from her books and a modest legacy. The farm was managed for her by John Cannon, who had the help and support of a wife. Hill Top was extended to separate the accommodation used by Beatrix from that of the farm manager and his wife. The house, owned by the National Trust, was opened to the public in 1961. It is visited by a vast number of people annually.

Holehird, above Windermere, where Beatrix stayed with her parents in the summers of 1889 and 1895. Part of her time was spent collecting fossils and fungi in the local woodlands. Today, Holehird is best known for its gardens, ten acres of which the Lakeland Horticultural Society leases from the Holehird Trust and maintains by voluntary labour.

Keswick. Beatrix was asked to judge at Keswick Show. She was an authority on Herdwick sheep and, in 1943, became President-elect of the Herdwick Sheepbreeders' Association. Alas, she never became President. Her death occurred before this distinguished honour could be bestowed on her.

Lakefield. A large house of the early Victorian period, it is prominently situated at Sawrey with a fine view of Esthwaite Water and its flanking hills. It was re-named Ees Wyke (house on the shore). The Potters stayed at Lakefield in the summer of 1896. It was here that Beatrix first discovered Hill Top Farm.

Lindeth How, in Storrs, outside Bowness, has a sweeping view of Windermere and a range of Lakeland fells. Beatrix bought the property in 1919 for her octogenarian mother. In her day the staff included four maids and two gardeners. A coachman was succeeded by a chauffeur

and mother regularly visited Beatrix at Near Sawrey. Rupert, Beatrix and her brother Bertram, stayed here in August, 1911. Mum led a somewhat isolated life. She had a cook and maids in the house. Also a favourite dog and canaries in cages that were set around her bedroom. Once a week, cook travelled in the chauffeur-driven car to town to obtain an apple – one apple cost one penny – for the canaries to nibble. Relations between Beatrix and her mother were strained, even though she had met her mother's day-to-day needs. When, occasionally, she went to Lindeth How, Beatrix had to walk to the ferry and, invariably, walk up to the big house on the hillside.

Lingholm, on a well-wooded, squirrel-haunted, western shore of Derwentwater. It was here, between 1895 and 1907, that Beatrix spent many summer holidays. One holiday was spent at adjacent Fawe Park. Lingholm was built in the 1890s. In the following decade, house and estate were purchased by the man who became Lord Rochdale. He developed the gardens and lakeside terrace. The garden became notable for its rhododendrons and azaleas. The vegetable garden in *The Tale of Peter Rabbit* was from paintings made at Lingholm. The woods and Owl Island (in reality St Herbert's Island) had a place in *The Tale of Squirrel Nutkin.* While staying at Fawe Park in the summer of 1903 Beatrix prepared *The Tale of Benjamin Bunny.*

Moss Eccles Tarn, which Beatrix acquired at the time of her purchase of Castle Cottage. The tarn was adorned by water lilies and on the banks are rhododendrons. Husband William Heelis, being keen on angling, the tarn was stocked with fish. They were "angled for" using a flat-bottom rowing boat that had its own little boathouse and is now preserved in a steamboat museum at Bowness.

Tarn Hows was part of the Monk Coniston Estate, of 4,000 acres, purchased by Beatrix in 1930 and donated to the National Trust. The road takes one-way traffic, with a parking place not far from the Tarn. The view of water and trees, with a backdrop of fells, has been frequently used to illustrate the beauty of Lakeland, though the scene is artificial. In the 19th century, three tarns were joined together by damming, the water benefiting industry in the valley. Most of the trees are upstart conifers. The combination of water, trees and a distant view

Autumnal study of Windermere, the largest lake in England.

of lordly fells accounts for the popularity of the area.

Newlands Valley. Newlands is easily approached from Keswick. A single range of hills separates the valley from Derwentwater. *The Tale of Mrs Tiggy-winkle* was based on Beatrix's pet hedgehog, an excellent "starcher", which she took with her on various trips. Mrs Tiggy-winkle had a home on the hill above the Newlands valley. Beatrix knew the Vicar of Newlands; she dedicated her story of Mrs Tiggy-winkle to Lucie Carr, the Vicar's daughter. Lucie's cottage is at Littletown, on the side of Catbells.

Troutbeck Park Farm, purchased by Beatrix in 1924. There was a possibility that the land might be bought for development. Beatrix was keen to see it retained for farming. Tom Storey was employed as shepherd for a year before moving to Hill Top, Sawrey, as farm manager. (He died in 1986, aged ninety).

Troutbeck Park, in a deep valley, with the road to Kirkstone Pass on the fellside high above, extends to 1,900 acres. Beatrix used the farm for the *Fair Caravan* stories; she also had a small room at the farm where she kept some of her minor possessions and where, occasionally, she would have a spell of writing.

The main buildings, having been whitened, gleam against the fields and the bulk of an isolated hill called The Tongue, where red deer are seen grazing in winter. Beatrix, visiting Troutbeck in a chauffeur-driven car, enjoyed sitting on the slopes of The Tongue enjoying the sights and sensations of Lakeland.

Windermere. The Potter family were photographed having a boating party on Windermere in September 1882. They were holidaymaking at Wray Castle. At Windermere town, The World of Beatrix Potter Attraction, described as "the only Beatrix Potter theme attraction in Europe," is on a grand, imaginative scale. Visitors are led, enchantingly, through a series of re-creations of the life and work of Miss Potter. The experience gives pleasure to all the senses – sight, sound, smells. Sculptures are also featured. The lighting effects are memorable. A visit, which is in six parts, and can take up to an hour, includes a Miss

Potter room containing aspects of biography. A shop and tearoom are also available.

Wray Castle. A castle in name only, accessed from the village of Wray. It may also be visited by motor launch from Waterhead Pier. Wray Castle, a private house in a Gothic Revival style, on the western side of Windermere, was constructed in the 1840s by Dr Dawson, a retired Liverpool surgeon, using money his wife had derived from a family business – in gin! It is now owned by the National Trust, who allow visitors to the grounds – which are adorned with fine specimen trees, including the mighty, soft-barked Wellingtonia – and sometimes, as announced, to the ground floor rooms of an unsuspectedly grand interior.

Rupert Potter arranged for a family holiday – mid-July to the end of October – in the year 1882. The Potters had normally visited Dalguise in Scotland, but this was no longer available. Beatrix was sixteen at the time. One of the Potter party at Wray was a spaniel, Spot, acquired during a Scottish holiday. Beatrix and her little brother Bertram enjoyed a walk from Wray Castle to Hawkshead. They repeatedly had to inquire about the way; they were barked at by collie-dogs at every farm, stuck in stiles and (once) chased by cows.

Dr Dawson also paid for the construction of nearby Wray Church. The incumbent at the time of the Potters' visit was Hardwick Rawnsley, who became a family friend. He was one of the founders of The National Trust. Wray Castle may, indeed, have been the place where what became the National Trust was conceived.

Yew Tree Farm, Coniston, dating from 1693. This was a traditional part of the Monk Coniston estate, which Beatrix, aged seventy, invited the National Trust to manage. Some of her furnishings have been retained in the house. There is a distinctive spinning gallery. Yew Tree Farm has guest accommodation.

Boats on Windermere.

Beatrix Potter and the National Trust

Conservation was a dominant interest of Beatrix Potter from her teenage years. Holidaymaking with her family, in 1882, she beheld a virtually unspoilt Lakeland landscape – and met a clergyman whose mission was, with others, to see it preserved from unseemly development. The Potter family took their holidays seriously, as well they might, for their holiday home – invariably a stately house – would be occupied for a month or more. In 1882, their choice fell on a "spoof" but imposing castle at Wray, its estate being lapped by Windermere.

Holiday was also show-off time. They were inclined to entertain local notables. At Wray, the guests included the local vicar, a bearded academic with the grand-sounding name of Hardwick Drummond Rawnsley. Ere long, he was commenting on the beauty of their surroundings and the need for it to remain unspoilt. Young Beatrix, having been impressed by Lakeland scenery, was moved by his conservation theme. And possibly, as an artist with an inclination to tell stories, by the fact that Rawnsley was the first published author she had met.

Rawnsley's mission, at Wray and later at Crosthwaite near Keswick, began with thoughts of a Lake District Defence Society. This eventually blossomed into a National Trust for Places of Historic Interest or Natural Beauty. It has been shortened to The National Trust. Rawnsley's life, which began in the South Country in 1851 and ended at Grasmere, heart of Lakeland, in 1920, had taken a turn through a family friendship with Tennyson. When he was at Balliol College, Oxford, he established a cordial friendship with John Ruskin.

In 1877, Rawnsley became vicar of Wray, near Ambleside. He married Edith Fletcher, of Ambleside. They had a son and called him Noel. Rawnsley took his parish duties seriously and also kept in mind the need to protect the countryside. Into being, initially, came the Lake District Defence Society. His conservation work had an instant appeal for Beatrix Potter, whose meticulous drawings, including those of animals with human traits, had greatly interested Rawnsley.

Back in London, Beatrix converted pictures into greetings cards and started a book which, with Rawnsley's enthusiasm, was published in 1902. This, her first book, became celebrated as The Tale of Peter Rabbit. For the publisher, Frederick Warne, it would be the literary equivalent of working a gold mine. A year after his first meeting with the Potters at Wray Castle, Rawnsley moved to St Kentigern's Church, at Crosthwaite.

The next few years were for him a time of feverish activity promoting notable schemes related to industrial art, farming, nursing and education - for the good of local communities. He became an Honorary Canon of Carlisle Cathedral in 1891. Rawnsley did not overlook the needs of the Lake District, challenging specific developments and crusading for an organisation that might preserve places of natural beauty and historic interest for the nation. This came to a joyful conclusion in 1895 when – with Miss Octavia Hill and Sir Robert Hunter – the National Trust came into being. Rupert Potter, the father of Beatrix, became the first life member.

Rawnsley, as Honorary Secretary up to his death over a quarter of a century later, led a money-raising campaign that funded the purchase of Brandlehow Wood, which was the Trust's first acquisition. After 34 years at Crosthwaite, Rawnsley retired to Grasmere, having purchased Allan Bank in 1915. He died there in 1920, bequeathing Allan Bank to the National Trust. The Times paid a fulsome tribute to his work: "It is no exaggeration to say...that England woud be a much duller and less healthy and happy country if he had not lived and worked."

Meanwhile, the conservation-minded Beatrix bought land of scenic importance, an example being Cockshott Point, on Windermere, the cost being met by the sale of fifty of her drawings. The most notable of many purchases came in 1930 when Monk Coniston Estate became hers. The 4,000 acres included Tarn Hows, which typified for many the splendour of Lakeland. It had, however, been tampered with by human kind, natural tarns having been dammed to create a lake and native trees taking second place to massed ranks of imported trees. At least the Lakeland theme is sustained by a dramatic backdrop of bare fells.

Display at Coniston
associated with the
film 'Miss Potter'.

The timely purchase and preservation of Lakeland farms that came up for sale and were in danger of being purchased for unseemly development brought Beatrix into regular business association with William Heelis, solicitor. They were married.

Beatrix was too busy to write much. She was concerned with the salvation of traditional Lakeland farming – the type that occurred at dale-country farmsteads where there were stocks of the indigenous sheep breed, the Herdwick. She found pleasure at traditional Lakeland shows, the first to take her fancy being in Eskdale. She was the first woman to be elected president-designate of the Herdwick Sheepbreeders' Association.

The National Trust sustains her work, having the top side of ninety farms and lots of Herdwicks in a total sheep population of 25,000. Beatrix Potter's benevolence towards The National Trust is inspiring. The office at Hawkshead where William Heelis, her husband, spent much of his working life has been preserved and tastefully adapted by the Trust under the title Beatrix Potter Gallery.

Miss Potter, a recent Beatrix Potter biopic, dealt movingly with the theme of preservation, taking in her early life in London, holidays in the Lake District – and the beginning of that new phase of life, as a Lakeland resident, anxious to continue her interests in superb surroundings.

I was pleased to see sequences at Yew Tree Farm, in the Yewdale valley near Coniston. That farm, like Hill Top at Sawrey, was once owned by Beatrix Potter. In the film Miss Potter it became a picturesque version of Hill Top. Beatrix would surely have approved the comment of Renée Zellweger, who played the part of Beatrix Potter: "I have been completely stunned by the beauty of the landscape and the tranquillity of the scene."

Also by W.R. Mitchell, available from Great Northern Books:

HANNAH HAUXWELL – 80 Years in the Dales

The Official Biography to Celebrate the 80th Birthday of this Remarkable Dales Character
Hannah captured the hearts of the nation when she was the subject of an extraordinary documentary, *Too Long a Winter*. The TV programme made her a national celebrity. Further programmes followed. She went on tours of Europe and America, shook hands with the Pope and played the piano on the Orient Express. This major book traces the extraordinary life of a delightful personality who has never lost her links with the dales countryside. It includes many previously unpublished photographs.
Fully illustrated. Hardback.

"Hannah Hauxwell should be an inspiration to us all." Daily Mail

THUNDER IN THE MOUNTAINS – The Men Who Built Ribblehead

The harsh, often violent, true story of those who built Ribblehead Viaduct, is related in this beautifully produced and fully illustrated hardback. For ten years, the railway settlement around Batty Green was home to hundreds of navvies, their wives and children, who experienced earthquake, flood and smallpox. Today, their monument is the landmark viaduct, carrying the much loved, Settle-Carlisle line.
Fully illustrated. Hardback.

"... factual accuracy with racy story-telling" Yorkshire Post
"This true-life drama is gripping from start to finish." Patrick Stewart

WAINWRIGHT – His life from Milltown to Mountain

Bill Mitchell was a great friend of the legendary walker and writer, Alfred Wainwright. In this ground-breaking, richly anecdotal and personal book about Wainwright, he recalls Wainwright's young days in the Lancashire milltown of Blackburn and his fascination – as a lone walker – for wild places in Lancashire, along the Pennines and in the north-west extremities of Scotland.

"I worked with AW on and off for five years but was still given a fresh glimpse of the great man in this smashing new book"
Eric Robson Chairman, Wainwright Society

Visit www.greatnorthernbooks.co.uk